Protecting Intellectual Freedom in Your Academic Library

Intellectual Freedom Front Lines

Protecting Intellectual Freedom in Your Academic Library: Scenarios from the Front Lines,
by Barbara M. Jones

Protecting Intellectual Freedom in Your Public Library: Scenarios from the Front Lines,
by Candace D. Morgan

Protecting Intellectual Freedom in Your School Library: Scenarios from the Front Lines,
by Pat R. Scales

Protecting Intellectual Freedom in Your Academic Library

Scenarios from the Front Lines

Barbara M. Jones

For the Office for Intellectual Freedom

AMERICAN LIBRARY ASSOCIATION

CHICAGO   2009

Sidebars on pp. 17, 38–39, 54–55, 94–95, 134–35, 154–55, 163, 165, and 168–69 by Deborah Caldwell-Stone.

The paper used in this publication meets the minimum requirements of American National Standard for Information Sciences—Permanence of Paper for Printed Library Materials, ANSI Z39.48-1992. ∞

Library of Congress Cataloging-in-Publication Data
Jones, Barbara M. (Barbara Minette), 1946–
    Protecting intellectual freedom in your academic library : scenarios from the front lines / Barbara M. Jones for the Office for Intellectual Freedom.
        p. cm. — (Intellectual freedom front lines)
    Includes bibliographical references and index.
    ISBN 978-0-8389-3580-4 (alk. paper)
    1. Academic libraries—Censorship—United States—Case studies. 2. Intellectual freedom—United States Handbooks, manuals, etc. I. American Library Association. Office for Intellectual Freedom. II. Title.
Z675.U5J72 2009
027.70973—dc22   2008046188

ISBN-13: 978-0-8389-3580-4

Printed in the United States of America
13 12 11 10 09   5 4 3 2 1

Dedicated to the librarians and staff at Virginia Tech Libraries, Blacksburg, Virginia

Ut Prosim (That I May Serve)

Contents

Barbara M. Jones is the Caleb T. Winchester University Librarian at Wesleyan University in Middletown, Connecticut. She received her M.L.S. from Columbia University in 1978 and her Ph.D. in history from the University of Minnesota/Twin Cities in 1995. She was added to the Freedom to Read Foundation Roll of Honor in 1999 and awarded the Robert B. Downs Intellectual Freedom Award for 2007. Jones wrote *Libraries, Access, and Intellectual Freedom* (American Library Association, 1995). Currently she serves as a U.S. representative and secretary to the Committee on Free Access to Information and Freedom of Expression Committee of the International Federation of Library Associations and Institutions. She conducts workshops worldwide on such issues as access to government information, the IFLA Internet Manifesto, and the librarian's role in providing access to public health information.

Acknowledgments

I wrote this book at Wesleyan University, Middletown, Connecticut. The First Amendment collections here are amazing, thanks to Leonard S. Halpert, class of 1944, who has endowed the library's Collection on Freedom of Expression. Thanks to the entire library staff for providing me with interlibrary loan and other services. Thanks to my wonderful boss, provost Joe Bruno, who continues to support my professional growth and interests. Thanks to Don Moon, dean of the College of Social Studies, John Finn, professor of government, and Judith Brown, professor of history, all of whom enjoy discussing these ideas and helped me clarify my thinking. Thanks to the Oberlin Group library directors, who provided so much feedback to my case studies. As always, I couldn't do this work without the terrific support from the ALA Office for Intellectual Freedom. Deborah Caldwell-Stone has worked on the sidebars and consulted with me on legal issues. I am especially grateful to my friends and traveling buddies on the IFLA/FAIFE Committee, particularly to Fatima Darries, Loida Garcia-Febo, Stuart Hamilton, Jassim Jorhees, Victoria Okojie, Marica Sapro-Ficovic, and Paul Sturges, from whom I've gained an international perspective on freedom of expression. And to my other IFLA colleagues whose friendship is a constant inspiration to me: Elizabet Carvalho, Lily Echiverri, Barbara Ford, Isabel da Franca, Alejandra Martinez, Felipe

Martinez, Marcia Rosetto, and Susan Schnuer. Thanks to my first group of students for the Intellectual Freedom 645 course, at University of Wisconsin–Madison's School of Library and Information Science, who are a constant inspiration.

Introduction

U.S. Higher Education in the Twenty-first Century

The library, in my opinion, is the only tolerant historical institution. . . . For it's a mirror of our society—the record of mankind. It is an institution in which the left and the right, the Devil and God, human achievements, human endeavors and human failures all are retained and classified, in order to teach mankind what not to repeat and what to emulate. . . . Cemeteries do not provide earthly immortality to men and women . . . but libraries can promise you immortality, and deliver it.

Vartan Gregorian, Librarian and President of the Carnegie Corporation of New York, speech at the dedication of the Middlebury College Library, October 8, 2004

At the same time Middlebury College is creating a stunning new library as a testament to the life of learning and critical thinking, U.S. higher education and its libraries face a sober beginning to the new century. Those academics who lived through the McCarthy era in the 1940s and 1950s recall that civil liberties and higher-education organizations lacked commitment to protect the besieged faculty, librarians, and administrations of that time. Although the U.S. Supreme Court later tried to rectify those oversights with increased constitutional protections, many contemporary academics believe that we still live in what law professor Geoffrey Stone calls "perilous times."[1] The USA PATRIOT Act, passed in the emotional aftermath of September 11, abridges the rights of faculty, students, and librarians by chilling library services and open access to information. Broadening wiretapping laws are compromising library user privacy in alarming ways.

Librarians must incorporate these issues of library intellectual freedom and professional ethical concerns into the broader campus discourse. To do this we must be at the table as colleges and universities shape their missions and priorities for the twenty-first century. Probably the most changed institution on any campus is the library. Other traditions and campus culture have arguably not kept up with the changing operational, financial, and other needs of the twenty-first-century library. Many campus decision makers have not done library research for a decade or more. They may have never used an electronic journal article or a blog.

Librarians must understand this environment because we have our work cut out for us in communicating our new priorities and mission and what we need to achieve our new vision. To do this well, we must understand the culture within which we work and the campus themes and issues facing colleges and universities as a whole. Only then can we set our strategic goals and uphold the professional principles of intellectual freedom—because they affect almost every corner of campus culture. The most dangerous error is to assume that campus libraries are a high priority and always will be, and that these very global library issues will be easily embraced and adopted. At the same time, librarians must understand the particular culture and issues on today's campuses, because we are an integral part of them.

CAMPUS CONSTITUENCIES

To understand issues of intellectual freedom particular to academic libraries, one must know the relations among the key players in an academic institution. Each of the constituencies below has specific interests, agendas, and research needs associated with the library.

Faculty

My experience—as a student, a librarian, and now the parent of a college student—is that the vast majority of faculty are dedicated to, and energized by, their teaching, research, and service—the three areas on which they are evaluated for tenure. Contrary to the opinion of some special interest groups, most faculty maintain and encourage a classroom atmosphere open to new ideas, critical thinking, and disagreements—and they truly agonize when students accuse them of acting otherwise. Faculty members form lasting relationships with some of their students and colleagues, including librarians. They evaluate papers and research projects carefully and use personal conferences, course management systems, e-mail, and good old-fashioned pencils to provide useful feedback. Many faculty volunteer on community service projects or serve on the city council. Most serve on college and library committees, even if, compared to research and publishing, these committees do not "count" much toward tenure. The U.S. professoriate is the envy of most students and faculty in other parts of the world, where the student/faculty relationship is more formal and resources scarce.

Most faculty care deeply about the library as a place for their students to work and for faculty to research and write that book required for tenure.

Incidentally, the same can be said for academic librarians.

Few academic librarians would disagree that any institution's *teaching faculty* is a primary constituency. (I use this italicized term to distinguish the academic disciplinary faculty from such other institutional faculty as librarians, who might also teach.) Although there is always much talk about the importance of student opinion and influence on campus, in fact faculty drive the agenda and priorities in most institutions. Faculty must be cultivated by librarians because they are important allies who can make or break a library's campus status and effectiveness.

Faculty are usually trusted library allies on issues of intellectual freedom because their research and teaching depend on an environment supportive of academic freedom. It is important for librarians to make them aware of how these principles affect librarians, services, new technologies, and collections. Most faculty will make this connection and support their library colleagues.

Professor Michael Bérubé of Pennsylvania State University is a well-regarded commentator and interpreter of the current status of the professoriate in regard to institutional citizenship and concern with issues of academic freedom. His book, provocatively titled *What's Liberal about the Liberal Arts? Classroom Politics and "Bias" in Higher Education,* is explored later in this chapter.

Another perspective is offered by Stanley Katz in "What Has Happened to the Professoriate?" Katz sees an unwieldy professoriate that lacks institutional loyalty or ties to the local community. Many are highly specialized and uninterested in teaching undergraduates. Katz opines:

> Academic freedom—the freedom to teach and to learn—is central. But it must follow from an acceptance of the duties of professionalism. We have such academic "rights" only if we embrace the duties of a public profession—to instruct the untrained and to create knowledge.

That includes the obligation to identify the standards by which practice can be assessed and to enforce adherence to them.[2]

Administration

Campus administrations provide institutional leadership, which includes managing the finances and setting priorities. They must weigh competing issues, and the library is usually not at the top of that list. We need not mention the very real threat of campus violence as witnessed in recent years. And there are other issues. For example, deferred maintenance of campus infrastructure may have rendered many buildings in dire physical condition. In such a case, the priority must be to fix temperamental elevators, not to increase the library acquisitions budget.

One key issue is the ever-sharpening divide between faculty and administration. Colleges and universities now face a more complex environment, which includes more bureaucracy to cope with corporate, parental, fiscal, and legal demands. In many cases administration has been "professionalized" because the jobs have become more complex than untrained, inexperienced faculty can handle.

Librarians must engage with administrators at every turn if they expect to be on the campus agenda. Administrators do not always understand how some issues affect libraries, and we must remind them. The common example librarians have all faced is that of adding ten new faculty lines without considering the impact on the collections/access budget. Inevitably at least some of these new faculty members will be disappointed to discover that the library does not have the materials or access to meet their needs. Even if the library has the resources to support the addition of new subject fields, it takes time to build expertise in the library to service students and faculty.

It is also important to understand that many administrators were told in the 1990s that libraries would become paperless. When librarians respond that this scenario did not and will not materialize and that, in fact, library costs continue to rise, administrators may be surprised or assume we have not done enough to cut costs.

State Legislature

Public higher-education institutions often get tossed about in the peaks and valleys of state funding, though even publicly funded colleges and universities get a high percentage of their funding from private sources these days. Communicating with local, state, and federal legislators is part and parcel of many academic librarians' assignments now. As Bérubé muses about the naïveté of the academic community in regard to lawmakers,

> I've often come away from these [faculty] debates wishing that these people would realize that the most vocal and stringent critics of American universities couldn't care less about the difference between traditional art history as practiced by Edwin Panofsky and eclectic postmodern art history as practiced by James Elkins. Sooner or later, I want to tell them, the right-wing state legislator is going to show up at the campus gates, flanked by his staff and a couple of hundred irate parents and local residents, demanding to know why "secular humanism" is so prevalent in American universities.[3]

Academic librarians have never been as active in library legislative matters as their public library colleagues. Activism for the Academic Bill of Rights (discussed below) is just one reason it is imperative for academic librarians to get more involved. The recently inaugurated Association of College and Research Librarians (ACRL) legislative initiative for academic librarians is a significant step in the right direction.

Board of Trustees

Boards of trustees wield a tremendous amount of power and influence over the goals, priorities, and fiscal policies of colleges and universities. Trustees are often alumni with strong institutional attachments. Sometimes they are political appointees, and their mission is biased by that obligation. Quite often they eventually move into the presidency of the institution. Trustees are often generous donors. Public library boards often get embroiled in traditional censorship issues; that is not typically the case in academe. Trustees have, however, been responsible for the approval and implementation of campus speech codes and for the removal of professors for ideological reasons. For the purposes of this book it is important for academic librarians to understand the makeup and dynamics of the board and to be alert to potential ideological conflicts. Boards of trustees play key roles that can enhance or compromise academic freedom.

Students

The student population on most U.S. campuses is more diverse than ever. One finds older second-career seekers; the "typical" millennial teenager; commuters; advanced-placement high school students; Elderhostel participants; international students; male, female, and transgender students; and students of every ethnic, economic, and religious background. Each student brings to college a unique library experience and technological proficiency (or lack thereof) necessary to navigate today's academic library. That is why information literacy programs must be tailored to meet the learning styles and research needs of so many types of students.

One characteristic of most groups of students is their growing technological skill. The *Library Journal* article "Born with the Chip" lists useful characteristics of these students: "nomadic, multitasking, experiential, collaborative, integrated, principled, format agnostic, adaptive, and direct."[4] OCLC has published a helpful report, *College Students' Perceptions of Libraries and Information Resources*, which empirically verifies the views of the *LJ* article.

One of the troublesome outcomes of this digital information environment is the lack of distinction between private and public electronic space. Millennial students' casual disregard for privacy sometimes returns to haunt them; the press has recounted stories of students rejected for jobs when prospective employers discovered unsavory content on the applicant's Facebook page. Regardless, today's college student freely associates with information, sorts it, sifts it, sends it on, and shares it without much thought about privacy or copyright. Another interesting outcome of the digital information age is the "self-service environment." These students may help themselves to Google information, unaware of the differences in accuracy, authenticity, and sources. College students still need someone to mediate information, and the library is the perfect place for such collaborations among students, faculty, and librarians. Here students can learn to discern among the various information sources and decide what suits their purposes best.[5]

A helpful source for understanding one large group of college students is *Millennials Rising: The Next Great Generation,* by Neil Howe, R. J. Matson, and William Strauss. Millennial students often study in groups and are given group course assignments. Thus academic libraries have added group study rooms and at the same time have tried to be sensitive to students' sense of privacy and personal space. Still, there is a great deal of evidence that privacy is not as important to these students as to their parents.

The millennials are much more likely to trust their government and those around them. Combined with the millennial student's love of group cohesiveness, there is evidence that today's college students do not value individualism as much as their parents' generation. A high percentage of these children wore uniforms to school.[6]

Most millennials are technologically savvy. Frances Jacobson Harris has written an insightful monograph about teenage Internet users, *I Found It on the Internet,* based on her experiences as the high school librarian at University Laboratory High School at the University of Illinois, where over 90 percent of the students are college-bound and will be the clients of academic librarians.[7] She notes several important study characteristics that have surely followed these kids into college. One is that students favor an "informal" information-seeking mode—that is, they open up their favorite websites or read RSS feeds. The information comes to them and they "sift and winnow." One thing leads to another; they do not perform a formal linear inquiry.

Today's information environment is nonhierarchical and matrix-like, says Harris. She cites the Pew Internet and American Life Project to show that teenagers and college students use the Internet more than they use the library for their school projects. This is not to say that the library does not provide Internet access. It means that students do not seek a mediated experience with a librarian to obtain information. Further, as librarians have feared, these students do not know how to select websites likely to have the most authoritative information.

Harris's survey of student use of information and communications technologies is excellent. Academic librarians need to understand how handheld devices and other technologies affect personal privacy as well as how they affect student information-seeking habits. And yet many high schools are banning social networking devices at the same time that college professors are podcasting their lectures. We are in a period of great excitement over the possibilities of new teaching and learning methodologies but at the same time are feeling anxiety over the potential harm that might come from these communications tools. For example, Harris discusses what she calls the "deep end," where students access content that might be illegal—such as child pornography. And though there is ample evidence of the entertainment and pedagogical value of computer games, some students can get "addicted" to them and isolate themselves socially in favor of friendship in the virtual world.

Information Technology Services

It is impossible for libraries to operate without a good relationship with the campus IT service, and vice versa. In some institutions the two departments are "blended." In either case, it is important to understand that the two cultures still differ in important ways.

As a profession, librarianship focuses on long-term stewardship of resources as well as on short-term activities and projects. The long view taken, for example, on the preservation of information may not be readily understandable to IT professionals who do not deal with special collections or the stewardship aspects of institutional heritage. Librarians also like to push the envelope when it comes to intellectual property and censorship. For example, they push fair use as far as they believe is legal in order to provide the best possible service to their customers. Librarians are also extremely concerned about privacy issues because of their professional code of ethics. Also, academic librarianship emphasizes quick turnaround and often customized services for their clients.

To be fair, in recent years IT departments have been far more focused on excellent *service* than in the past. Also, because some information content is now created digitally on campus, it can be argued that IT is now involved with content and not just with the hardware and software that delivers it. Some IT professionals, especially in academic computing, probably have just as much contact with faculty and students as librarians do and are equally concerned with good service. And IT professionals argue that they can turn around a service far more quickly than the library, which tends to study potential changes far longer than is practical in the twenty-first century.

As a rule, IT professionals are more focused (as they must be) on the careful monitoring of institutional digital resource costs than on providing increased, unfettered access. They may be more risk averse as a result, in the interest of fiscal responsibility. This is not to say that librarians and IT professionals have totally different orientations. On most campuses there is, thankfully, a great deal of common ground. For example, both groups understand the important changes in information delivery and in scholarly communication. Institutional repositories, as well as the management of other content such as visual resources, are often joint projects between IT and the library. Such joint projects save duplication of precious campus resources.

But when it comes to issues of intellectual freedom, that particular professional value may be lacking in the IT professional's education and training. Librarians should make sure that, when collaborative projects are undertaken or campus decisions made about network access, such values as privacy and open access to information are presented. In this crucial IT/library relationship, librarians may well need to create awareness of these issues and explain their relevance.

Alumni and Other Donors

Academic institutions are increasingly sensitive to the wishes and feelings of their major donors. Libraries almost always depend on endowed funds to supplement their acquisitions budgets. And dedicated alumni are often the "movers and shakers" of the Library Friends group. Still, I have heard of situations in which donors are reluctant for books with gay or lesbian themes to be purchased from their funds; I have also heard of development offices pressuring libraries to accept endowment restrictions that would hinder public access to such material. Librarians with fund-raising responsibilities need to anticipate these types of problems. They may well need to explain to an alumna why the library supports a particular controversial exhibition or spends so much money on a particular type of publication. Many librarians have turned down gifts with too many strings attached. To refuse a gift requires that the library have the support of the development office and other key players before a controversy begins.

General Community and Taxpayers

Most academic institutions seek alliances with their local communities for purposes of economic development and cultural collaboration. In Connecticut, Yale and Wesleyan universities are two examples of institutions deliberately creating stronger community bonds; both were previously perceived as turning their backs on New Haven and Middletown, respectively. Public higher education understands that state legislatures expect results from institutional research paid for by the taxpayers. Farmers look to their state university to provide them with research to help increase their crop yields. Libraries are a key component in this research delivery chain. Statistics show that colleges and universities often reside in the most politically liberal areas of their state. Thus some campus administrators need to work hard to demonstrate to the legislators that campus expenditures reflect the needs of the state and are not liberal "ivory towers." As we see in chapter 2, conflicts can sometimes arise when libraries or campuses select books or expose students to ideas that threaten some elements of the state's population.

Academic Librarians: What Does the Campus Think of Us?

Former ACRL president Pamela Snelson has thought a lot about the perceived value of academic librarians. In a 2006 article she tells how she discovered that academic libraries have not clearly articulated their value.[8] She contracted the Library Research Center at the University of Illinois at Urbana-Champaign to conduct phone interviews with chief academic officers. So far twenty-six interviews have been conducted, and these provosts have advised librarians to be more aggressive in asking for resources. This report will be completed in 2008/9. I maintain that reluctance to act as advocates extends to our reluctance to promote intellectual freedom. We should not assume that everyone on campus is going to agree with us—or, on the other hand, that advocating intellectual freedom is a hopeless task.

Regardless of how our academic colleagues view us, librarians must understand that not all components of the campus are going to support the principles of intellectual freedom, because they may have equally compelling and conflicting agendas. Also, campus administrations are more risk averse than ever, given incidents of campus violence and the events of September 11. Lynn Sutton's presentation to the tenth national ACRL conference explains:

This was driven home to me in a recent example on our campus involving a death threat to a professor made from one of the library's public workstations. I sat in a room with the Chief of Public Safety, the university's Legal Counsel and the Vice-President for Computing and Information Technology. It struck me, as we each made our respective cases, that we all had a territory to protect: the policeman felt he had to protect the physical safety of the individuals in his jurisdiction, the lawyer felt he needed to protect the legal and economic liability of the university, the computer professional felt he had to protect the security of the network, and I felt it my professional honor and obligation to protect the First Amendment rights of all library users. They wanted the library to immediately begin authenticating every user on every library computer, to use static, rather than dynamic IP addresses for easier tracking, to maintain extensive "history" and "cache" files on every computer and to turn them over [to] the authorities on demand. I had to remind them that under Michigan's Library Privacy Act, it would be against the law for library staff to turn over personal identification information without a court order, even to them. When they didn't believe me, I had to call on the ALA Office for Intellectual Freedom and ALA's legal counsel to back me up. Eventually, we agreed to work out a university policy for future cases, but the point is, what if I were not in the room?[9]

Sutton makes several crucial points: First, librarians are often *not* in the room. This is a significant problem that ACRL is addressing head-on in its advocacy initiative. Second, campus officials—even the campus counsel—are not well versed on library law. This has been proven time and time again in my career. This lack of campus expertise in First Amendment law as applied to libraries underscores the importance of ACRL's current campaign to make academic librarians an integral part of the campus culture so that their voices are heard and respected.

CURRENT THEMES

Now that we have been introduced to the key players, let us turn to the issues that keep us up at night. They are shared by all to some degree, and they are related.

Academic Freedom

> We could not for a moment think of recommending the dismissal or even the criticism of a teacher even if some of his opinions should, in some quarters, be regarded as visionary. Such a course would be equivalent to saying no professor should teach anything which is not accepted by everyone as true. This would cut our curriculum down to very small proportions. We cannot for a moment believe that knowledge has reached its final goal, or that the present condition of society is perfect. We must therefore welcome from our teachers such discussions as shall suggest the means and prepare the way by which knowledge may be extended, present evils be removed and others prevented. . . . In all lines of academic investigation it is of utmost importance that the investigator should be absolutely free to follow the indications of truth wherever they may lead. Whatever may be the limitations which trammel inquiry elsewhere we believe the great state University of Wisconsin should ever encourage the continual and fearless sifting and winnowing by which alone the truth can be found. (University of Wisconsin Trustees, 1894)[10]

The idea of academic research, teaching, and learning as a "sifting and winnowing" process captures the essence of the college and university library mission. It places librarians and libraries at the center of academic life. Traditional libraries facilitated student and faculty browsing the shelves for books and journals. Library users have now added the Internet and other social networking communication to the scholarly process of sifting and winnowing. In the twenty-first-century academic library, faculty, students, and librarians are partnering to identify, provide access to, and mediate the discovery process in a world with more information than ever. The academic library's growing emphasis on information literacy means that librarians are doing more classroom-style teaching and collaboration with faculty and students. Principles of academic freedom thus apply to librarians' work, which increasingly mirrors that of teaching faculty. That is why many colleges and universities afford faculty status to librarians.

Academic freedom is a European concept, codified in the United States in 1915 with the American Association of University Professors' (AAUP's) "Declaration of Principles." This milestone document called for "freedom of inquiry and research; freedom of teaching within the university or college; and freedom of extra-mural utterance and action." Today's updated "1940 Statement of Principles on Academic Freedom and Tenure" can be found at www.aaup.org, a valuable website that documents all sides of the current academic freedom debate—from Michael Bérubé to David Horowitz.

The *Sweezy v. New Hampshire* (1957) decision was a significant but only partial endorsement of academic freedom. The Supreme Court suggested that faculty in higher education are afforded First Amendment protection from legislative inquiry into classroom content. Although *Sweezy* and other cases bolstered academic freedom, the courts did not construct a concise relationship between academic freedom and the First Amendment until 1967 (see Focus box opposite).

Principles of intellectual freedom in the library and the traditional concept of academic freedom differ somewhat, but they share roots. An academic library lacking a supportive campus culture in regard to academic freedom will have trouble protecting

Academic Freedom and the First Amendment

The U.S. Supreme Court first recognized academic freedom as a liberty deserving constitutional protection in *Sweezy v. New Hampshire.* Sweezy, an instructor at the University of New Hampshire, refused to answer a state attorney general's questions about the content of his lectures, and the state supreme court found him in contempt of court. The Supreme Court overturned his conviction, declaring that the attorney general's inquiry constituted an invasion of Sweeney's liberties in regards to academic freedom and political speech. In describing the nature of the protected liberty interest, the Court stated that

> The essentiality of freedom in the community of American universities is almost self-evident. No one should underestimate the vital role in a democracy that is played by those who guide and train our youth. . . . Scholarship cannot flourish in an atmosphere of suspicion and distrust. Teachers and students must always remain free to inquire, to study and to evaluate, to gain new maturity and understanding; otherwise our civilization will stagnate and die.

In a concurring opinion, Justice Felix Frankfurter identified the four essential freedoms of the university: "to determine for itself on academic grounds who may teach, what may be taught, how it shall be taught, and who may be admitted to study."

Though *Sweezy* acknowledged the importance of academic freedom, it did not explicitly associate academic freedom with the First Amendment. A decade after its decision in *Sweezy,* the Supreme Court squarely placed academic freedom among the recognized rights protected by the First Amendment in *Keyishian v. Board of Regents.* The plaintiffs in *Keyishian* challenged a New York law that required college faculty to sign a loyalty oath and forswear membership in "subversive organizations." The Court overturned the law on the grounds that the statute infringed on faculty members' academic freedom and freedom of association.

In extending First Amendment protection to academic freedom, the Court stated:

> Our Nation is deeply committed to safeguarding academic freedom, which is of transcendent value to all of us and not merely to the teachers concerned. That freedom is therefore a special concern of the First Amendment, which does not tolerate laws that cast a pall of orthodoxy over the classroom.

Courts since have protected universities from government and political interference, deferring to the institution's decision making concerning faculty, curriculum, academic standards, grading, and similar academic functions. For example, in *Linnemeir v. Board of Trustees, Indiana University-Purdue University, Fort Wayne,* and *Yacovelli v. Moeser,* courts dismissed attempts by taxpayers, legislators, and students to prevent the use of controversial instructional materials in the college curriculum.

Additional Resources

Keyishian v. Board of Regents, 385 U.S. 589 (1967)
Linnemeir v. Board of Trustees, Indiana University-Purdue University, Fort Wayne, 260 F.3d 757 (7th Cir. 2001)
Sweezy v. New Hampshire, 354 U.S. 234 (1957)
Yacovelli v. Moeser, 324 F. Supp. 2d 760 (D.N.C. 2004)

the intellectual freedom of its users. Thus academic librarians have sought common ground with faculty and administration by linking the shared values of intellectual and academic freedom. ACRL has linked academic librarianship to academic freedom, and the relationship between academic freedom and library intellectual freedom has been endorsed by the AAUP. In 1972 a joint committee of ACRL, the Association of American Colleges (AAC), and the AAUP drafted the "Joint Statement on Faculty Status of College and University Librarians." In addition to supporting faculty status for librarians, the statement upholds academic freedom for librarians:

> College and university librarians share the professional concerns of faculty members. Academic freedom, for example, is indispensable to librarians because they are trustees of knowledge with the responsibility of insuring the availability of information and ideas, no matter how controversial, so that teachers may freely teach and students may freely learn.[11]

Similarly, in the 2002 document "Guidelines for Academic Status for College and University Librarians," ACRL explicitly extends academic freedom to all academic librarians, including those without faculty status.[12] ALA maintains an "Academic Freedom" section searchable on its website, which contains current documents and issues from ALA, the AAUP, the Center for Campus Free Speech, and related organizations. Also included are documents about the current Academic Bill of Rights controversy (discussed below).

Although academic freedom is the "common ground" concept shared by academic librarians, faculty, and others on campus, intellectual freedom as formulated by the library profession differs somewhat. Academic institutions, both private and public, usually guarantee academic freedom through faculty handbooks, student codes of conduct, or collective bargaining agreements—through contractual relationships rather than exclusively through constitutional rights. Guarantees of academic freedom are usually restricted to the rights of faculty to determine what goes on in their classroom, including course content. On many campuses students are included in the campus academic freedom statement. First Amendment scholar Robert O'Neil summarizes:

> Academic freedom as a constitutionally protected interest did not, of course, evolve in a vacuum. Its emergence was accompanied by several other complementary developments. Notably, the First Amendment says nothing about the right to associate, affiliate, or belong. It does mention "freedom . . . peaceably to assemble," but this is about as close as the text comes. It was not until 1958, in fact, that the Supreme Court first recognized as necessarily implicit within the First Amendment a right to associate with others for political purposes and, as a corollary, the right not to be forced to divulge an unpopular affiliation. . . . Not long after recognizing freedom of association and entertaining loyalty oath challenges, the Supreme Court began to curb a governmental power that was even more central to McCarthyism, by restricting the scope of legislative inquiries into political beliefs and associations.[13]

On the other hand, principles of library intellectual freedom are more closely tied to First Amendment rights, which are guaranteed only in public institutions. Many states have, however, passed laws—like California's 1992 Leonard Law—that afford speech protection to those working in private institutions.[14] A recent court case has muddied the waters even further, but for now the Supreme Court seems to be keeping academic freedom in a special protected category, even as it questions the right of other public workers to exercise their First Amendment rights in the workplace.[15]

Academic Freedom at the Dawn of a New Century is the published proceedings of a February 2004 conference sponsored by Loyola Marymount University and the

Institute for Leadership Studies.[16] In his introduction, Matthew J. Streb summarizes the major themes, all of which necessarily affect academic library collections and services. He uses the phrase "the Debate over Education vs. Indoctrination" to frame the current debate over the nature of teaching and learning—how much should a professor's (or a librarian's, by extension) personal or scholarly biases enter into classroom teaching (or library collections and services)?

Benno C. Schmidt Jr., former president of Yale University and currently chairman of the board of trustees for the City University of New York, asserted in a 1991 speech: "The most serious problems of freedom of expression in our society today exist on our campuses. . . . the assumption seems to be that the purpose of education is to induce correct opinion rather than to search for wisdom and to liberate the mind."[17]

Schmidt's quotation is commonly used on both the right and the left of the U.S. political spectrum to justify various political agendas in higher education. For example, Schmidt is cited by the American Council of Trustees and Alumni (ACTA, www.goacta.org). Founded in 2005 by chair of the National Endowment for the Humanities Lynne V. Cheney, former Colorado governor Richard D. Lamm, Connecticut senator Joseph I. Lieberman, social scientist David Reisman, and Nobel laureate Saul Bellow, ACTA aims to "uphold high academic standards, safeguard the exchange of ideas on campus, and ensure that the next generation receives a philosophically balanced, open-minded, high-quality education at an affordable price." The current ACTA leadership—Jerry L. Martin and Anne D. Neal—believe that colleges and universities are not providing students with a diversity of views. ACTA issued reports that caused a firestorm in higher-education circles: "Intellectual Diversity: Time for Action" in 2005 and "How Many Ward Churchills?" in 2006—both available on the ACTA website. ACTA believes that a diversity of views is no longer encouraged or tolerated in the college classroom. Rather, it asserts that liberal and radical leftist politics dominate and students feel intimidated to express opposing beliefs. Interestingly, to date ACTA has not accused libraries of biased collections.

In 2006, David Horowitz, a self-proclaimed conservative activist, founded the David Horowitz Freedom Center (www.horowitzfreedomcenter.org), formerly the Center for the Study of Popular Culture. Part of this organization's activity is carried out by Students for Academic Freedom (www.studentsforacademicfreedom.org), which recruits students to monitor college classroom sessions for bias. Sara Dogan's *Students for Academic Freedom Handbook* (which can be downloaded from the website) contains a complaint form students can use to report professors violating academic freedom—for either not presenting a diversity of views or preventing students from expressing opposing views. For example, one of the boxes students may check on the form is "Mocked national political or religious figures." Both organizations are promoting an Academic Bill of Rights (ABOR), for which they are lobbying in state legislatures. The entire text of the proposed bill can be found on Horowitz's website. Two of its principles are as follows:

> Curricula and reading lists in the humanities and social sciences should reflect the uncertainty and unsettled character of all human knowledge in these areas by providing students with dissenting sources and viewpoints where appropriate.
>
> Exposing students to the spectrum of significant scholarly viewpoints on the subjects examined in their courses is a major responsibility of faculty. Faculty will not use their courses for the purpose of political, ideological, religious, or anti-religious indoctrination.[18]

At first glance some of the ABOR statements sound somewhat like the ALA's Library Bill of Rights, which has always advocated that library collections and services represent a diversity of viewpoints. It is important, though, to understand the distinctions between the two documents. Horowitz's organization is lobbying for state legislative oversight of course content and faculty appointments, in order to ensure intellectual diversity on campuses. That is why ALA joined higher-education organizations in opposing the ABOR. Passed in January 2006, an ALA Council resolution argues that academic institutions—without government oversight—have already established their own structures for grievances, promotion, and tenure and that the ABOR creates unnecessary, extra-academic standards. The resolution also reaffirms that academic libraries "guarantee that a wide array of ideas that promote academic discourse are available."[19] Unlike ALA's stance on diversity of views in a library, the ABOR is seeking legislative approval for what is viewed by ALA and such groups as the AAUP as ideological control of the classroom. Diversity of views, these latter groups argue, is a value that should not be legislated. The ABOR guidelines would measure diversity by means of political standards, not by academic criteria. The AAUP maintains that students' papers and exams must be graded according to scholarly standards, not by student or faculty political beliefs or beliefs that cannot be backed up in the scholarly documentation of the subject field. The ABOR, in contrast, assumes that all knowledge is uncertain, when in fact some discoveries have been widely accepted by broad consensus in the scholarly community—for example, that certain scholarship about Shakespeare is better researched and more fundamental than other scholarship. The AAUP has always maintained that faculty must have at least a modicum of authority over the classroom; after all, they do assign grades on the basis of professional judgment. Further, it argues that there are already numerous statements from within the higher-education community condemning faculty indoctrination of students, so legislation is not needed. Finally, student grievance procedures are already in place in most colleges and universities.[20] The AAUP statement "Proposed Government Oversight on Teaching and Learning" was updated in March 2007 in the face of at least ten pending proposals in state legislatures. As of August 2008, no state has approved the ABOR.

Responding to the pressure from various sectors of higher education, the Association of American Colleges and Universities (www.aacu.org) issued a 2006 report, "Academic Freedom and Educational Responsibility." Its findings are so relevant to academic library services that they are included here, from the section "What Is Not Required in the Name of Intellectual Diversity?"

In an educational community, freedom of speech, or the narrower concept of academic freedom, does not mean the freedom to say anything that one wants. For example, freedom of speech does not mean that one can say something that causes physical danger to others. . . . Students do not have a right to remain free from encountering unwelcome or "inconvenient questions," in the words of Max Weber. . . . Students do have a right to hear and examine diverse opinions, but within the frameworks that knowledgeable scholars—themselves subject to rigorous standards of peer review—have determined to be reliable and accurate. That is, in considering what range of views should be introduced and considered, the academy is guided by the best knowledge available in the community of scholars. . . . All competing ideas on a subject do not deserve to be included in a course or program. . . . For example, creationism, even in its modern guise as "intelligent design," has no standing among experts in the life sciences because its claims cannot be tested by scientific methods. However, creationism and intelligent design might well be studied in a wide range of other disciplinary contexts such as the history of ideas or the sociology of religion. . . . While the diversity of topics introduced in a particular area of study should illustrate the existence of debate, it is not realistic to expect that undergraduate students will have the opportunity to study every dispute relevant to a course or program. The professional judgment of teachers determines the content of courses.[21]

Though using different terminology, the AACU report also has much to say about "sifting and winnowing" that will surely resonate with academic librarians specializing in information literacy:

> Although one often hears that faculty "impart knowledge" to students, the reality is that, in a good liberal education, substantial time is devoted to teaching students how to acquire new knowledge for themselves and how to evaluate evidence within different areas of knowledge. To do this well, professors in the classroom also need academic freedom to explore their subjects—including contested questions and real-world implications—with their students. . . . To develop their own critical judgment, students also need the freedom to express their ideas publicly as well as repeated opportunities to explore a wide range of insights and perspectives.[22]

Horowitz denies that he is calling for the firing of liberal professors or seeking political control over the curriculum. He maintains that he has created awareness of a problem and points to the fact that Temple University is the first institution to add "students" to its now titled "Student and Faculty Academic Rights and Responsibilities."[23]

But the debate rages on, echoing the 1990s "culture wars" in higher education. Michael Bérubé, professor of English at Pennsylvania State University, recently published the provocative *What's Liberal about the Liberal Arts?* When his own state legislature created a House subcommittee on academic freedom in response to Horowitz's ABOR, Bérubé's writings reaffirmed the AAUP position that the ABOR cedes control of higher education to the government. Citing several examples from his own classroom experiences at the University of Illinois and Pennsylvania State University, Bérubé wrote of his struggles to keep his classroom free of personal biases and open to a diversity of views. His book opens an important window into typical faculty/student relationships in a large twenty-first-century state university—complete with state legislative pressures, racial and ethnic tension, and students of every political stripe and economic status.

In a 2006 blog posting, Bérubé looks more deeply at the conservative accusation that the academy is too biased toward the left. He uses recent statistics to argue that the academy, indeed, has always been left-leaning, but not as liberal as conservatives would have us believe. His analysis cites Higher Education Research Institute statistics from 1989 to 2001/2. Of 55,000 faculty members from 416 institutions, the categories "liberal" or "far left" grew from 45 to 48 percent during that period. In some academic fields there are more conservatives than liberals. Currently, only 18 percent of the general public describe themselves as liberals—a percentage that has remained steady since the Vietnam War era. And so, though it is probably true that the academy has always had more liberals than are found in the general public, students still have at least a 50 percent opportunity to get one or the other.[24]

Students, too, are challenging the ABOR initiative. The Center for Campus Free Speech (www.campusspeech.org) is one example of a student "push-back" site.

Libraries, of course, are affected by the debate about academic freedom in terms of collections, information literacy instruction, and reference services; it has been argued that even a book's classification within a call number structure is an ideological act. Academic librarians need to monitor this ongoing discourse, because Horowitz's group could easily decide to target academic library collections and instruction. If that should happen, ALA's carefully articulated policies regarding balanced collections and services will be extremely useful tools.

September 11

The September 11, 2001, attack on the United States, along with the related economic slowdown, continues to haunt higher education. The negative impact on endowments and state funding affected all academic operations, including libraries. Foreign students, librarians, and faculty from certain countries or cultures continue to encounter barriers against entering the United States. Ironically, as a result of the political aftermath of September 11, U.S. higher education is now challenged to preserve the very academic freedom that makes it the best system in the world. At the same time, academe faces government pressure for more antiterrorism surveillance on campus operations—even when such surveillance compromises individual privacy and the tradition of unfettered scholarly discourse.

The balancing act between two important government policy initiatives—privacy on the one hand and government oversight during times of war on the other—has already forced campuses to adopt poorly thought-out, uncoordinated policies that often inadvertently affect academic library collections and services. Robert O'Neil, director of the Thomas Jefferson Center for the Protection of Free Expression at the University of Virginia, also heads up the AAUP's Special Committee on Academic Freedom and National Security in Time of Crisis. He reminds us that the USA PATRIOT Act and other government surveillance measures are responses not unlike Sen. Joseph McCarthy's response to the Communist threat in the 1950s. During that time almost seventy tenured or tenure-track professors were dismissed for suspicious activities. O'Neil documents several post–September 11 attempts to dismiss or censure faculty for remarks that were deemed insensitive or treasonous by students or legislators; most of these cases have been settled. O'Neil documents three instances that were probably resolved in favor of academic freedom only because certain administrators were in the right place at the right time. One was Lee Bollinger, president of Columbia University, where Professor Nicholas De Genova held teach-ins and made provocative statements about Israel and his wish for "a million more Mogadishus," referring to the defeat of the U.S. Army during urban warfare in the capital of Somalia. Columbia alumni from around the world demanded that De Genova be dismissed, but Bollinger resisted. O'Neil concludes that academics have much more protection from their peers, the public, and the courts than during the McCarthy era. For example, the AAUP now has the committee chaired by O'Neil; during McCarthyism it did not.[25]

The PATRIOT Act's significant impact on libraries is covered in chapter 5. It affects not only libraries but also faculty hires. It denies entry to the United States to any person who has funded a terrorist organization, and the definitions of such organizations are very broad. In 2004 the University of Notre Dame hired Tariq Ramadan with a tenured appointment. Because of his financial connections to a Palestinian charity that may have supported Hamas, Professor Ramadan was denied entry. Other academics have been turned away for "irresponsible expressions of opinion."[26]

And the PATRIOT Act is only one post–September 11 law affecting freedom of expression in academe. The Communications Assistance for Law Enforcement Act (CALEA) and Family Educational Rights and Privacy Act (FERPA) are other laws with specific applications to academic libraries. O'Neil may well be correct in his assessment that academics have more protections in place today than during McCarthyism, but it is also true that in the 1950s law enforcement did not have today's expansive powers of electronic surveillance.

Campus Civility Issues and Speech Codes

Another challenge facing campus leaders is balancing freedom of speech with the assurance of a safe and supportive learning community for all, regardless of religious or ethnic background. Many campuses attempted to address this problem with campus speech codes, which generally prohibit speech that is racist, sexist, homophobic, or demeaning to any established religion. The motive for such codes is to create a campus atmosphere of tolerance, diversity, and comfort.

Such codes, of course, highlight a conflict that often arises between freedom of speech and civil rights—something libraries struggle with when particular content is offensive to particular groups protected by civil rights law. In an early case, *Doe v. University of Michigan* (721 F. Supp. 852 [E.D. Mich., 1989]), a federal district court declared the university's "Policy on Discrimination and Discriminatory Harassment of Students in the University Environment" to be unconstitutional because it was "overbroad." This legal terminology refers to laws or policies that cast too wide a net; that is, the law or policy might legitimately prohibit speech that is not protected by the First Amendment but, with too wide a net, inadvertently prohibit speech that is protected. As an example, library filtering software is often overbroad in blocking content that is constitutionally protected for adults. Overbreadth was the reason the courts ruled Stanford University's speech code unconstitutional in 1995.

Donald Alexander Downs's *Restoring Free Speech and Liberty on Campus* provides valuable insight into the evolution of the University of Wisconsin's failed attempts to create a campus speech code.[27] One should be aware that in academic institutions efforts to block free speech could well arise from the political left. When Donna Shalala became Wisconsin's chancellor in 1988, she was determined to create a campus more tolerant of diversity. A faculty code and a student code were adopted in 1988/89. The student code punished any student for

> racist or discriminatory comments, epithets or other expressive behavior directed at an individual or on separate occasions at different individuals, or for physical conduct if such comments, epithets or other expressive behavior or physical conduct intentionally: 1. Demean the race, sex, religion, color, creed, disability, sexual orientation, national origin, ancestry or age of the individual or individuals; and 2. Create an intimidating, hostile or demeaning environment for education, university-related work, or other university-authorized activity.

The faculty code was similar but incorporated protection of academic freedom. However, it contained definitions and burdens of proof for determining whether the expressive behavior was punishable.

In 1990 the student code was challenged, and in 1991 the district court ruled that the code violated the First Amendment because it was overly broad. Eventually the faculty code was abolished and the student code repealed, after the Supreme Court's ruling in *R.A.V. v. City of St. Paul* (505 U.S. 377 [1992]) made it clear that even the revised student code would not pass constitutional muster.

It is often the case that speech highly offensive to some is nonetheless protected by the First Amendment. Speech that could lead to violence ("fighting words") and certain libelous and slanderous speech are not protected. In recent years, however, the courts have been gradually narrowing the definition of "fighting words." For example, recent rulings tend to protect posters and even verbal attacks against particular groups—at either public or private universities. First Amendment rights appear to trump any perceived harm to these groups. Furthermore, the courts have ruled that speech codes place the burden on the academic institution to prove that such codes will actually "result in a change of atmosphere and belief." Otherwise, the courts argue, it is wrong to have a law that chills speech because it does not even address the problem it was designed to solve. In fact, after such cases as the previously mentioned *R.A.V. v. City of St. Paul* and *Wisconsin v. Mitchell* (508 U.S. 476 [1993]), the current campus wisdom deems it practically impossible to write a speech code that will pass constitutional muster. The ACLU and similar free speech groups advocate that campuses look, instead, to

> stress the means they use best—to educate—including the development of courses and other curricular and co-curricular experiences designed to increase student understanding and to deter offensive or intolerant speech or conduct. These institutions should, of course, be free (indeed encouraged) to condemn manifestations of intolerance and discrimination, whether physical or verbal.[28]

The essential role of libraries as campus public forums and repositories of knowledge that generate understanding must not be lost here.

Assessment and Measurement

One need only glance at the website of the Middle States Commission on Higher Education (www.msche.org), or any of its sister agencies, to understand the high priority of assessment in academe today. MSCHE's 2008 workshop offerings are almost exclusively devoted to institutional and instructional assessment issues. As MSCHE president Jean Morse states clearly in her "Overview of U.S. Institutional Accreditation," accreditation standards

> emphasize results instead of processes. The emphasis on learning outcomes is greater than that on institutional resources such as physical plant and library holdings. . . . information literacy

is emphasized over library resources. Whether the graduate can research and communicate is more important than the size of the library.[29]

Clearly, when campus officials seek foundation support, reaccreditation, or legislative increases in the campus budget, they understand that academic activities must be presented and documented in terms of empirically measured outcomes. Academic librarians would do well to consult the website of their school's regional accrediting agency years before they are required to write the self-study for the visiting team.

How did we end up in this assessment environment? Many assign responsibility (or blame) to Margaret Spellings, the U.S. Secretary of Education when she formed the Commission on the Future of Higher Education in 2005 to examine the state of higher education. When the nineteen-member commission submitted its 2006 report, there was great consternation in academe, especially about the report's assertion that "there is a shortage of clear, comprehensive, and accessible information about the colleges and universities themselves, including comparative data about cost and performance." The report further stated that

> a robust culture of accountability and transparency should be cultivated throughout the higher education system, aided by new systems of data measurement and a publicly available information database with comparable college information. There should also be a great focus on student learning and development of a more outcome-focused accreditation system.[30]

As higher education competes for ever scarcer resources, and the general public continue to be wary of what they view as a liberal bias, scrutiny by government agencies is likely to continue.

Academic libraries are part of this accreditation process, and ACRL and ARL have responded to this assessment challenge. I was recently contacted by NELINET to participate in a regional assessment modeling workshop, so that the New England region librarians could prepare for upcoming self-studies. ACRL's January 2007 *Environmental Scan* responds to the Spellings report:

> Higher education will be increasingly viewed as a business, and calls for accountability and for quantitative measures of library contributions to the research, teaching, and service missions of the institution will shape library assessment programs and approaches to the allocation of institutional resources. . . . Now the belief that higher education must begin to produce tangible evidence that it is committed to improving student learning and achievement has become very important and widespread among universities. . . . Schools (and libraries) will have to demonstrate in a more quantitative way that they have had a positive impact on student graduation rates, retention, and transfers.[31]

The campus culture of assessment is anathema to some who believe that what is so special about the best colleges and universities is intangible. Indeed, that is the most often heard response of loyal (and often deep-pocketed) alumni. Regardless, institutions are being challenged to measure how the professoriate is spending its time—in state universities, for example, whether their research is supporting state economic development.

Such an atmosphere can easily lead to scrutiny of library acquisitions budgets. It can also lead to challenges from legislators over freshman orientation reading lists (see chapter 2). Libraries have always assessed their collections and made careful choices about what to buy (because there has never been enough money to buy everything). But the new kinds of assessment could easily lead to more scrutiny over purchases considered pornographic, works by such academics as Ward Churchill (see chapter 1), or science collections that are biased toward evolution and global warming (or intelligent design, depending on the particular campus culture). In this book I emphasize the importance of campus librarians taking a preemptive, proactive stance—of articulating the library's contribution toward overall campus excellence, measured empirically. Increasingly librarians will be at the table with colleagues from different departments and will be expected to assess, promote, and defend their activities and budget requests in ways that can be understood by all at that table. As a colleague at the University of Illinois used to advise librarians, "Be able to justify library costs to the football coach, to the Affirmative Action officer, to an undergraduate, and to a professor of soybean biology—all in the same room at the same time."

Finances

Just as university endowments were beginning to recover from the bursting high-tech bubble and the post–September 11 financial declines, along came the current threat of recession. In 2006 the Council of Higher Education Management Associations surveyed its membership about future threats to excellent higher education. Over 40 percent of respondents viewed "insufficient financial resources to meet future strategic objectives" as one of the top three threats, and 25 percent of respondents viewed the securing of those resources as one of the top three issues commanding their energies.[32] The often fierce campus competition for scarce resources continues; ACRL and other library organizations are offering advocacy skills training so that librarians can triumph in the fray.

For years now academic library budgets have been gutted by price increases in journals and other information products. Budget crises have already necessitated the cutting of low-use library materials. The last desperate measures often involve cutting titles from the alternative presses, newer experimental publications lacking an academic track record, and controversial materials that become harder to defend when dollars are scarce. Library budget cuts do not directly lead to censorship, but they certainly have tempted librarians to avoid controversial purchases in favor of those with broader appeal. There is also the likelihood that campus fund-raisers will buckle under pressure from wealthy donors over campus controversies—which have often included book purchases.

Academic librarians must be strong advocates for consistent funding increases. Because academic libraries did not traditionally need to fight as vociferously for dollars, some of us did not learn the advocacy skills necessary in the current contentious environment. Today's senior campus administrators are less likely to view the library as a "protected" resource; instead, libraries are more likely to be viewed as a fiscal "black hole." For the library profession, which is historically risk averse, these battles for funds can be very uncomfortable.

But librarians must become advocates for the cultural and intellectual legacy we protect and promote. The academic library is a place where students can explore information for the sheer joy of the chase—without a faculty member observing or a course syllabus requiring. A student with an independent study project or a senior thesis can work with a librarian to assemble books, journals, blogs, artists' books, and other information crossing traditional disciplinary lines for what might be a highly individualistic project. In other words, students can explore ideas in an academic library, with librarians to support them when they want help and to protect their privacy when they want to be left alone.

As library budgets shrink, the intellectual diversity of collections is threatened. Librarians have taken creative, bold steps toward creating new economic models for scholarly communication. These models support breadth, depth, and diversity of information and encourage access to increased resources through consortia.

ACRL understands these economic pressures and has produced a tool kit to assist academic librarians in fighting for their piece of the pie. This "must read" resource is *The Power of Personal Persuasion*.[33]

Lawsuits and Aversion to Risk

Funding shortages have made academic institutions even more risk averse. This means that, when a campus is faced with an intellectual freedom challenge, librarians may have more difficulty defending freedom of expression when the campus must protect ever-shrinking resources. This happened on many campuses recently when faced with implementing CALEA or copyright infringement threats. In the case of CALEA, campuses are far more likely to interpret "incidental use" of campus computer terminals strictly and thus lock down all terminals previously open to public access—even if the FCC has yet to hand down specific guidelines. After all, the recording industry has made good on its promise to sue students for downloading music, and expensive lawsuits loom large. It makes the courage of the Connecticut librarians who challenged the PATRIOT Act (see chapter 5) all the more notable, when one considers that boards of trustees are far less likely to expose themselves to risk over intellectual freedom issues these days. And, of course, librarians who do not hold tenured or permanent employment may be risk averse—at the very time when they need to be bold and creative in promoting access to a diversity of ideas.

Public and Private Institutions: Differences That Matter to Their Libraries

Academe, of course, includes both public and private institutions. There is a great deal of misunderstanding over the differences between these two in reference to intellectual freedom. One of the best comparative analyses can be found in *The First Amendment on Campus: A Handbook for College and University Administrators.*[34] Although this book does not include specific references to libraries, its chapter 3 compares public and private institutions in terms of legal status, with citations of key court cases. Public colleges and universities are government entities and thus must operate in accord with the U.S. Constitution, including the First Amendment. Public higher education is governed by federal, state, and local legislation as well as by such agencies as the FCC. Students and faculty at public institutions thus have rights guaranteed by the Constitution and applicable federal, state, and local laws. So, for example, if a state passes a law on confidentiality of library records, all public institutions as defined in that law must comply. Libraries in publicly funded institutions are also subject to the *public forum doctrine* (see chapter 4). Many libraries in private institutions follow state privacy statutes, but not because they are legally bound to do so. They may choose to adopt state library confidentiality policies on the basis of professional ethical values. The same is true of decisions about library collections.

Private institutions have *contractual* obligations with their students and their faculty. Guarantees of academic freedom and freedom of expression are often stated in faculty and student handbooks, which are contractual documents. That is why librarians in both private and publicly funded institutions must become familiar with the content of these handbooks. Many institutions have written documents outlining the status of librarians, which should contain the same guarantees as those for faculty freedom of expression, given that principles of intellectual freedom govern every aspect of library work and decision making.

To summarize, the First Amendment protects individuals from government interference. Public colleges and universities, as government entities, must not interfere with such individual rights. At a private institution, the institution has the freedom to define its mission however it wishes.

Most private colleges and universities do adopt the values of the First Amendment and academic freedom, so librarians are often surprised that they are not legally required to follow state confidentiality statutes. Many private institutions would be hard pressed to get the kind of faculty, librarians, students, and administrators they desire if privacy rights and academic freedom were abridged. For librarians in private institutions, it is crucial to understand the culture of academic freedom of your particular college or university. Some librarians might not be happy working in a private institution that abridges freedom of speech—as is their right. On the other hand, many librarians are distressed that public university libraries protect speech that goes "over the line" for many sensibilities, even if that speech is protected by the First Amendment.

There is a misconception that any institution receiving federal funds becomes a government entity and therefore is subject to First Amendment scrutiny. This is not the case. As the authors of FIRE's guide state, "Accepting federal funds usually makes the university subject only to the conditions—sometimes broad, sometimes narrow—explicitly attached to those specific programs to which the public funds are directed."[35]

State Actors, Private Actors, and the First Amendment

As government-owned and government-funded institutions, public universities and colleges are *state actors,* whose activities are controlled by the First Amendment of the U.S. Bill of Rights. The First Amendment generally limits the ability of state actors to regulate or impair fundamental free speech rights, including free expression, free association, religious freedom, and the separation of church and state. A library operated by a public university or college is therefore subject to the body of First Amendment law that addresses academic freedom, censorship, free inquiry, and the ability to access spaces and facilities designated for public use.

Private universities and colleges that are not controlled or funded by the government are *private,* or *nongovernmental, actors.* Private actors are not, in general, subject to the First Amendment, which protects only against speech limitations imposed by state actors (though private institutions may become subject to government regulation by accepting government funding or by agreeing to comply with government accreditation standards). Private universities and colleges can, and often do, protect free speech rights on campus through private policy or contract. Institutions accomplish this by adopting policy statements like the ALA Library Bill of Rights or the AAUP Statement on Academic Freedom, or by incorporating explicit protections for academic freedom into employment contracts.

Neither the U.S. Constitution nor the Bill of Rights prevents individual state governments from granting greater expressive rights, however. A 1980 Supreme Court decision, *Pruneyard Shopping Ctr. v. Robins,* held that the state courts could interpret the free speech provisions in their state constitutions as guaranteeing greater rights than those established under the First Amendment. States are thus free to protect speech activities taking place on private property or under the control of private institutions if their constitutional provisions grant a broader right to free speech than the First Amendment.

In the wake of the *Pruneyard* decision, only a handful of states took steps to restrict the ability of private actors to regulate free expression under the provisions of their state constitutions. Among these are New Jersey and California, whose courts and legislatures have moved to protect certain categories of free speech activities on the private university campus.

New Jersey's supreme court took the lead in 1980, when it overturned a pamphleteer's trespassing conviction for handing out political literature on the campus of Princeton University without permission. The court's decision in *State v. Schmid* held that, when a private actor has extended an invitation to the public to use its property in a manner "suitable for free speech," the New Jersey state constitution protects individuals from unreasonably restrictive or oppressive conduct on the part of the private actor that abridges the individual's right of free expression.

California's legislature sought to protect students' free speech rights when it adopted Cal. Ed. Code §94367, the "Leonard Law," in 1992. The Leonard Law, named for its sponsor, requires private universities to abide by the First Amendment as well as Article I, section 2, of the California Constitution, which protects free expression in that state. The law specifically prohibits private, postsecondary educational institutions from disciplining students for expressive activity that would be protected by the First Amendment outside of the institution. A California superior court relied on the Leonard Law to strike down Stanford University's speech code in 1995.

New Jersey and California remain part of a decided minority. Most states do not recognize a right to free expression on private property or require private actors to comply with a state constitution's free speech guarantees. Most state courts that have considered the question conclude that the state constitution operates only to constrain state action. Libraries in private universities and colleges that want to ensure intellectual freedom in the library can do so by adopting binding policies that protect free inquiry, the right to receive information, and the right to privacy.

Additional Resources

California Education Code §94367 ("The Leonard Law")

Corry v. Leland Stanford Junior University, No. 740309 (Cal. Super. Feb. 27, 1995) (striking down Stanford University's speech code) available on the Internet at www.ithaca.edu/faculty/cduncan/265/corryvstanford.htm.

Pruneyard Shopping Ctr. v. Robins, 447 U.S. 74 (U.S. 1980)

State v. Schmid, 84 N.J. 535 (N.J. 1980)

OUTLINE OF THIS BOOK

This book now proceeds with five chapters that explain, in real-world, practical terms, how academic librarians can promote their professional values on an operational level, within a campus context that is not always responsive to or aware of the ideals of intellectual freedom.

Each of these chapters covers an important issue of intellectual freedom for academic libraries. Each includes case studies, practical advice on addressing the issues using written policies, and landmark legal decisions informing the ALA policy stance on various issues.

Chapter 1 moves from general issues of academic freedom on campus to intellectual freedom in academic libraries. Topics include the role of intellectual freedom in planning library physical space, with emphasis on the importance of written policies in such initiatives as scholarly communication, information literacy, and technological and digital innovation.

Chapter 2 is about collections. Today, academic library "collection" is really any and all information to which a library can get access for its user community. It includes content on a physical shelf, content on a virtual shelf, content that is borrowed from a shelf at another university, and content that is created and stored in an institutional repository. Do the rules for collection development apply to all formats and to all forms of access? Is user privacy protected in all cases?

Chapter 3 is about Internet access. Although it is true that the collections discussed in chapter 2 include Internet content, chapter 3 focuses more on Internet service and privacy issues. Do the traditional library use policies apply, even when the medium of communication is as powerful, as pervasive, and as "in your face" as the Internet?

Chapter 4 celebrates the academic library as agora—a marketplace of ideas. It discusses the use of academic libraries as a public forum—with exhibits, lectures, and performances. It explains the public forum doctrine and how to write policy in a way that promotes the lively use of library spaces in an equitable and legal way.

Chapter 5 addresses the increasingly urgent issue of privacy. How has technology brought this issue to the forefront of concern not only for the general public but also for libraries? How can libraries balance user privacy rights with the values of open access?

This book demonstrates, through examples and case studies, how upholding intellectual freedom in academic libraries is ultimately rewarding, promotes the very highest quality of library service, and need not lead to disaster but, instead, to deeper campus understanding of the issues.

NOTES

1. Geoffrey Stone, *Perilous Times: Free Speech in Wartime: From the Sedition Act of 1798 to the War on Terrorism* (New York: W. W. Norton, 2004).
2. Stanley B. Katz, "What Has Happened to the Professoriate?" *Chronicle of Higher Education,* October 6, 2006, B11.
3. Michael Bérubé, *What's Liberal about the Liberal Arts? Classroom Politics and "Bias" in Higher Education* (New York: W. W. Norton, 2006), 99.
4. Stephen Abram and Judy Luther, "Born with the Chip," *Library Journal,* May 1, 2004, 34–37.
5. OCLC, *College Students' Perceptions of Libraries and Information Resources* (Dublin, Ohio: OCLC, 2005). www.oclc.org/us/en/reports/perceptionscollege.htm.
6. Neil Howe, R. J. Matson, and William Strauss, *Millennials Rising: The Next Great Generation* (New York: Vintage, 2000).
7. Frances Jacobson Harris, *I Found It on the Internet: Coming of Age Online* (Chicago: American Library Association, 2005).

8. Pamela Snelson, "Communicating the Value of Academic Libraries," *College and Research Libraries News,* September 2006, www.ala.org/ala/mgrps/divs/acrl/publications/crlnews/2006/sep/valueacademiclibraries.cfm.

9. Lynn Sutton, "Advocacy for Intellectual Freedom in an Academic Library," paper delivered at the ACRL Tenth National Conference, March 15–18, 2001.

10. Theodore Herfurth, "Sifting and Winnowing: A Chapter in the History of Academic Freedom at the University of Wisconsin," in *Academic Freedom on Trial,* ed. W. Lee Hansen (Madison: University of Wisconsin Press, 1998), 58–59.

11. ACRL, "Joint Statement on Faculty Status of College and University Librarians," 1972, reaffirmed by the ACRL Board, June 2001, www.ala.org/ala/mgrps/divs/acrl/standards/jointstatementfaculty.cfm.

12. ACRL, "Guidelines for Academic Status for College and University Librarians," 2002, www.ala.org/mgrps/divs/acrl/standards/guidelinesacademic.cfm.

13. Robert O'Neil, "Academic Freedom in the post–September 11 Era: An Old Game with New Rules," *Academic Freedom at the Dawn of a New Century: How Terrorism, Governments, and Culture Wars Impact Free Speech,* ed. Evan Gerstmann and Matthew J. Streb (Stanford, Calif.: Stanford University Press, 2006), 56.

14. www.leginfo.ca.gov/cgi-bin/displaycode?section=edc&group=94001-95000&file=94367.

15. See www.insidehighered.com/news/2006/05/31/supreme.

16. Matthew J. Streb, "The Reemergence of the Academic Freedom Debate," in Gerstmann and Streb, *Academic Freedom,* 3–16.

17. Benno C. Schmidt Jr., "The University and Freedom," speech at the 92nd St. YMCA, New York City, March 1991, 1, 3.

18. Articles from the "Academic Bill of Rights," developed by the Students for Academic Freedom, posted on their website: www.studentsforacademicfreedom.org. Specifically, see Sara Dogan, *Students for Academic Freedom Handbook,* 22–23, 62. This book can be downloaded at the website.

19. ALA, "Resolution in Support of Academic Freedom," January 2006, www.ala.org/ala/aboutala/offices/oif/statementspols/ifresolutions/academicfreedom.cfm.

20. AAUP, "Academic Bill of Rights and Intellectual Diversity," www.aaup.org/AAUP/GR/ABOR/.

21. Association of American Colleges and Universities, "Academic Freedom and Educational Responsibility," www.aacu.org/about/statements/documents/academicfreedom.pdf.

22. Ibid., 4–5.

23. David Horowitz, "After the Academic Bill of Rights," *Chronicle of Higher Education,* November 10, 2006, B20.

24. Michael Bérubé, "Academic Freedom," Friday, January 27, 2006, on *Le Blogue Bérubé,* www .michaelberube.com/index.php/academic_freedom/. Higher Education Research Institute statistics from www.gseis.ucla.edu/heri/faculty.html.

25. O'Neil, "Academic Freedom in the post–September 11 Era," 43–60.

26. George Packer, "Keep Out," *New Yorker,* October 16, 2006, 59–60.

27. Donald Alexander Downs, *Restoring Free Speech and Liberty on Campus* (Oakland, Calif., and Cambridge, Mass.: Independent Institute and Cambridge University Press, 2005).

28. ACLU website, www.aclu.org/Studentsrights/expression/12808pub19941231.html.

29. Jean Morse, "Overview of U.S. Institutional Accreditation," Middle States Commission on Higher Education, found at www.msche.org/?Nav1=ABOUT&Nav2=FAQ&Nav3=QUESTION01, 4–5.

30. "Highlights of the Final Report of the Secretary of Education's Commission on the Future of Higher Education," September 2006, www.ed.gov/about/bdscomm/list/hiedfuture, then click on September 2006 prepublication report.

31. ACRL, ACRL Research Committee, *Environmental Scan* 2007 (Chicago: American Library Association, 2008), www.ala.org/al/mgrps/divs/acrl/publications/whitepapers/Environmental _Scan_2.pdf.

32. Philip J. Goldstein, *The Future of Higher Education: A View from CHEMA* (Washington, D.C.: Council of Higher Education Management Associations, 2006), 8–9.

33. ACRL, *The Power of Personal Persuasion: Advancing the Academic Library Agenda from the Front Lines,* 2005/6, www.ala.org/mgrps/divs/acrl/issues/marketing/advocacy_toolkit.pdf.

34. Lee Bird, Mary Beth Mackin, and Saundra Schuster, eds., *The First Amendment on Campus: A Handbook for College and University Administrators* (Washington, D.C.: National Association of Student Personnel Administrators, 2006).

35. David French, Greg Lukianoff, and Harvey Silverglate, eds., *FIRE's Guide to Free Speech on Campus* (Philadelphia: Foundation for Individual Rights in Education, 2005), 58.

CHAPTER 1

Academic Libraries and Intellectual Freedom in the Twenty-first Century

Libraries must assert their evolving roles in more active ways, both in the context of their institutions and in the increasingly competitive markets for information dissemination and retrieval. Libraries must descend from what many have regarded as an increasingly isolated perch of presumed privilege and enter the contentious race to advance in the market for information services—what one participant in our roundtable termed "taking it to the streets."

The Power of Personal Persuasion, ACRL Toolkit, 2007

In addition to the *Power of Personal Persuasion* cited in the epigraph above, another must-read for all academic librarians is the recently published *Changing Roles of Academic and Research Libraries* (February 2007), available from ACRL at www.ala.org/acrl/. This report states what is really happening in academic libraries—now and for the foreseeable future. Much of this activity is not understood by the academic administrators to whom we report or from whom we request funds. Many administrators, after all, have not used a library for academic research since the digital revolution.

Intellectual freedom values are implicit and integral to each section of the report. With contributors from a variety of academic enterprises, *Changing Roles* accurately describes the dramatic changes in twenty-first-century libraries. The bottom line is now truly the bottom line—that is, libraries are no longer viewed as indispensable:

> In redefining and reasserting their value, libraries will have to embrace much more aggressively the fact that they are one of many contenders for their institution's financial support. Libraries have been comparatively slow to realize and accept the need to function in an environment of direct competition for resources, either from within or outside their institutions.

Academic libraries are moving from the traditional "book box" building focused on physical collections to a service-intensive, access-based model that delivers information to users quickly. This information may come from local shelves or the Web, other libraries, or consortia. It requires librarians to work closely with students on information literacy, to help them navigate through the overload of information—some reliable, some not. The ACRL document goes on to discuss negotiation and collaboration with other campus constituencies. All of this means that librarians should not talk just among themselves. The library profession has its own ethics and culture, which most of us absorb from attending meetings with other librarians and reading library websites and journals. We now must engage with campus players who do not know this culture. For example, many of us have had the experience of talking with campus police, who are surprised that librarians do not want them to tap students on the shoulder if they are viewing what police define loosely as "porn." Another common example is that IT staff may not understand user privacy the way the library professional does.

The focus of *Changing Roles* is, in short, advocacy. Many of us were not alerted in library school to the academic world of politics and competition. The academic library was once safely ensconced as the intellectual center of campus. This is no longer the case, even in the most privileged and heavily endowed institutions. We need to make our case clearly and regularly, to a diverse audience.

Advocacy of intellectual freedom and awareness of its issues can sound like the usual left-wing ideology to administrators unless librarians express these principles as essential to the academic mission. We need to craft our message carefully and not assume that everyone will be sympathetic. For example, faculty may at first not understand that, when they monitor their students' individual reading habits via a course management system, campus librarians are concerned. But when this surveillance of student reading habits is linked to academic freedom and other student privacy laws, faculty usually make the connection and support the campus library's patron privacy policies.

GENERAL THEMES IN ACADEMIC LIBRARIES

The Academic Library as Place

Some of the most exciting and creative work in academic libraries involves defining the space occupied by what is called the campus library. On many campuses the administration has called a moratorium on dedicating additional prime real estate for the storage of infrequently used books. Such collections are now stored off-site so that the main library space can be used for group study, social interaction, civic discourse programming, information literacy courses, and other user-centered activities and services.

Carleton College librarian Sam Demas describes academic library activity based on his own empirical study. He believes that student library use transcends technology issues. Students come because libraries "offer security, comfort, and quiet; are free and commercial free; provide a place to be with other people in a learning/cultural environment; offer opportunities to learn, search, inquire, and recreate; and afford opportunities for choice and serendipity."[1]

Library architect Geoffrey Freeman explains it this way:

> The library is the only centralized location where new and emerging information technologies can be combined with traditional knowledge resources in a user-focused, service-rich environment that supports today's social and educational patterns of learning, teaching, and research. Whereas the Internet has tended to isolate people, the library, as a physical place, has done just the opposite. Within the institution, as a reinvigorated, dynamic learning resource, the library can once again become the centerpiece for establishing the intellectual community and scholarly enterprise.[2]

Libraries are no longer "book boxes" but rather what the *New York Times* characterizes as "places to see and be seen." Freeman goes on to describe other aspects:

> The library is an intellectual marketplace. . . . Look at the souks in Middle Eastern marketplaces, where all the wares are out in the open. . . . I want to see the service points, the collections, see other people producing and doing things. I want to see activity, not rows of quiet tables.[3]

Those librarians who have created learning commons and other types of social spaces in their libraries are generally thrilled by the results. Nevertheless, the increased use of libraries for social purposes raises all sorts of privacy issues. Most librarians believe that the privacy problems can be solved and would not trade their new social spaces for the traditional model. But in designing such spaces one must remember that privacy screens may be optimal for workstations arranged close together. This is but one example of how every aspect of academic library activity—including space design—relates to issues of intellectual freedom. Also, one must consider how restrictions on time, place, and manner (see chapter 4) may affect exhibit and performance spaces in your library. Social space in academic libraries encourages deliberative democracy as well as academic discourse, discovery, and sharing of ideas. Study is no longer solely an individual endeavor. It involves faculty, student, and librarian collaborations—often with interactive resources. This is a good thing, but it brings up all sorts of issues related to freedom of speech, because such spaces beg for speech—and get it in spades.

Information Literacy

What used to be called "bibliographic instruction" and was experienced by many students as meaningless treasure hunts and other "library games" during freshman week has been totally transformed in recent years, thanks to the development of *information literacy* as a serious pedagogical program in the library profession. The ACRL website has comprehensive documentation of its excellent information literacy program. The information literacy pedagogical model has encouraged librarians to collaborate more closely with campus teaching faculty and to incorporate learning styles and outcomes into their work. Many academic librarians, of course, hold faculty rank themselves.

Librarians must ensure that their information literacy sessions offer students diverse perspectives. Like teaching faculty, librarians could well be vulnerable to criticism from activist groups if they offer what some view as only one view or the "politically correct" version of a controversial topic. For example, on the topic of global warming there are certainly a diverse number of views in the published literature, but many academic libraries buy or recommend only those materials that have been peer reviewed or recommended in review sources. Many academic libraries, including mine, include books that challenge the concept of global warming—even though Wesleyan has a Nobel laureate faculty member who has done distinguished work in that field. Students learn through their coursework and information literacy sessions how to judge for themselves.

Scholarly Communication

Scholarly communication is a new term for the ancient practice of researching, creating, publishing, and disseminating scholarship. All academic libraries are currently working on a set of activities usually related to this field. These include creating institutional digital repositories for scholarship created by faculty and students on a particular campus and dealing with a host of intellectual property challenges brought forth by the particular problems in a digital environment. The phenomenal rise in cost of scholarly journals has led to the open-access movement, encouraging faculty to retain their copyrights and publish in free, peer-reviewed, publicly accessible web journals.

As the field of scholarly communication continues to develop, it is clear that there are numerous intellectual freedom issues contained within its initiatives. Institutional repositories are subject to the same privacy issues as other library resources. Today's intellectual property laws, which increasingly restrict open access, are prompting many First Amendment experts to consider the chilling effect of copyright. And the prohibitive costs of library materials have a direct impact on academic library access and services.

I intend to monitor the area of scholarly communication and publish a separate work on its relationship to intellectual freedom in the near future.

The Role of Technology and Digitization in Academic Libraries

Ohio academic libraries founded OCLC in 1967. Since its beginnings, OCLC has promoted the latest digital technologies in the cause of sharing and preserving library resources. The development of Web 2.0 has dramatically changed campus teaching and learning activities. Library websites encourage communication through wikis, blogs, and electronic live reference services. All these developments have made it possible for libraries to move toward the goal of seamless access to information in a variety of formats.

Accompanying this exciting environment are challenges related to privacy, diversity in collection development, and intellectual property. Although librarians typically promote "fair use" as much as possible, there is considerable—and growing—pushback from the information providers. And when so much content is being exchanged on the Internet, the government has greater potential to wiretap and intrude on personal privacy.

In chapter 5 we closely examine the challenges and opportunities of an information world with the potential of promoting the equitable flow of information but at the same time compromising the privacy of its users. Librarians need to be at the table whenever campus decision makers tackle these complex and ever-changing policy issues.

INTELLECTUAL FREEDOM IN ACADEMIC LIBRARIES

The Current Status of Intellectual Freedom in Academic Libraries

Many academic librarians still view intellectual freedom as an issue primarily for public and school libraries. And some campus administrators do not understand intellectual freedom beyond the traditional issues of censorship. Meanwhile, the international and national library communities have moved decisively to include economic issues, privacy, and a host of other issues under the umbrella of intellectual freedom or freedom of expression. ACRL was the last ALA division to create its Intellectual Freedom Committee, in the 1990s. Since then, the divisional intellectual freedom committees have created invaluable policies and made a much-needed impact on ACRL and ALA, but there is much left to be done.

The ACRL Intellectual Freedom Committee began working on "Intellectual Freedom Principles for Academic Libraries" in 1998. This document was approved in 1999 and adopted by the ALA Council as an interpretation of the Library Bill of Rights on July 12, 2000. The AAUP endorsed it on November 11, 2000. Some of the key principles are noted below:

The general ALA Library Bill of Rights can be applied to academic libraries.

Privacy of users and confidentiality of a variety of library transactions are priorities.

Collection development should include access to a variety of points of view. This is a particular challenge when shrinking academic library budgets may force many academic libraries to buy only what is important to the curriculum and borrow the rest. Although this borrowing is increasingly essential, librarians should try to achieve a modicum of balance in content.

Preservation of print and other resources is a key component in preserving diversity of points of view through the ages. In academic libraries materials are often placed in special collections or in restricted areas to prevent wear and tear. If library budgets ignore the preservation of materials, they will disappear and valuable segments of our cultural heritage will be lost forever.

Licensing agreements are part of the everyday life of serials librarians. These agreements can be negotiated with intellectual freedom principles in mind, so that user access can be maximized.

The Internet in academic libraries should be unfiltered. This is an ideal to which all libraries can aspire, but it is particularly important to academic

Yale University Library's Confidentiality of Library Records Policy

Here is an example of a policy based on professional ethics, not on state confidentiality laws. This shows how libraries in private institutions can still promote patron privacy.

Confidentiality of Library Records

Librarians' professional ethics require that personally identifiable information about library users be kept confidential. This principle is reflected in Article III of the Code of Ethics, which the American Library Association adopted in 1981 and 1995 to guide librarians in making ethical decisions. Article III states: "We protect each library user's right to privacy and confidentiality with respect to information sought or received and resources consulted, borrowed, acquired or transmitted."

In order to protect the rights of individuals using Yale University Library material, electronic products and services, all circulation, collection registration, and/or use files are private and confidential records.

Under no circumstances may staff release the name of a reader to whom a book is charged, who is using a computer on library premises, or who has used any other library services. All staff, circulation and reference procedures, and automated systems will handle the recall of books from a reader, the identity of borrowers, and the profile of an individual's search for information, in such a way that confidentiality of records is maintained.

All requests for confidential information that cannot be handled through service procedures or any questions concerning this policy should be referred to an Associate University Librarian or University Librarian. As appropriate, Library Administration will consult with the University's General Counsel.

04/01/82 LMC revision 5/22/02

The Right to Receive Information

The First Amendment protects more than the right of free speech. It also protects other activities that are essential to the exercise of free speech that are not explicitly stated in the First Amendment. Among these is the right to receive information.

The Supreme Court first discussed the right to receive information in *Martin v. Struthers,* a 1943 decision that addressed the right to receive pamphlets from a person going door to door in a company town. In upholding the right of the town residents to receive the pamphleteer's brochures, the court held that "the right of freedom of speech and press has broad scope. . . . This freedom embraces the right to distribute literature, and necessarily protects the right to receive it." The Court's subsequent opinion in *Griswold v. Connecticut* further developed the contours of the right to receive information, identifying "the right to receive, the right to read and freedom of inquiry" among the rights protected by the First Amendment.

In 1965, Justice William Brennan elaborated on the basis for extending constitu-tional protection to the right to receive information:

> The protection of the Bill of Rights goes beyond the specific guarantees to protect from Congressional abridgment those equally fundamental personal rights necessary to make the express guarantees fully meaningful. I think the right to receive publications is such a fundamental right. The dissemination of ideas can accomplish nothing if otherwise willing addressees are not free to receive and consider them. It would be a barren marketplace of ideas that had only sellers and no buyers. (*Lamont v. Postmaster General*)

A lawsuit challenging a local school board's decision to remove several books from its high school library resulted in *Board of Education v. Pico,* a seminal 1982 Supreme Court opinion that explicitly recognized the right to receive information in a library. Observing that the First Amendment plays a role in protecting the public's access to discussion, debate, and the dissemination of information and ideas, the Court held that "the right to receive ideas is a necessary predicate to the recipient's meaningful exercise of his own right of speech, press and political freedom." It further identified the school library as the principle locus of the student's freedom "to inquire, to study and to evaluate."

The analysis used in the *Pico* decision provided the foundation for another court opinion that firmly identified the public library with the right to receive information. That opinion, *Kreimer v. Bureau of Police,* did not directly concern the receipt of information; instead, it addressed the decision by a public library to ban a homeless man from the library. But in order to determine whether the library's actions were consistent with the Constitution, the Third Circuit Court of Appeals was required to decide whether or not the homeless man's expulsion implicated the First Amendment.

The Third Circuit Court of Appeals ruled that government actions that deny access to the public library do raise First Amendment concerns. In its opinion, it stated that "the First Amendment does not merely prohibit the government from enacting laws that censor information, but additionally encompasses the positive right of public access to information and ideas"; this right necessarily includes "the right to some level of access to a public library, the quintessential locus of the receipt of information."

The constitutional framework established by the *Pico* and *Kreimer* court opinions continues to provide crucial protection for the right to receive information and the right to access information in the publicly funded library. Courts across the country have drawn upon this framework to return banned books to library shelves and to uphold principles of fair access in the library, providing direction to those responsible for developing intellectual freedom policies for libraries everywhere.

Additional Resources

Griswold v. Connecticut, 381 U.S. 479 (1965)
Kreimer v. Bureau of Police, 958 F.2d 1242 (3d Cir. 1992)
Lamont v. Postmaster General, 381 U.S. 301 (1965)
Martin v. Struthers, 319 U.S. 141 (1943)

libraries, where research must be unfettered and controversial topics must be explored.

Library exhibits and policy documents must reflect intellectual freedom principles (see chapter 4).

Policies for library meeting rooms and other facilities must also incorporate intellectual freedom principles.

There must be due process for any actions regarding removal of library resources, exhibits, or services. This includes any blocking of access for students who are suspected but not yet convicted of violating copyright laws by downloading music or videos.

Finally, it is important to obtain endorsement of the "Intellectual Freedom Principles for Academic Libraries" from the parent institution, through a faculty senate vote or similar means.

Academic libraries are not usually affected as much by traditional censorship as public libraries are. Most courts and pressure groups are willing to give more leeway to higher education, because some otherwise objectionable books can be excused as necessary for research purposes. The users of academic libraries are more likely to be young adults than young minors. Thus it is far more likely that privacy issues based on the wide use of technology for a variety of academic purposes will be the major intellectual freedom issue in higher education rather than the removal of books from the shelves.

Finally, academic libraries are global in their reach. Not all resources can cross national borders easily, however; a variety of national laws prohibit even certain categories of Internet content. Issues of international freedom of expression are thus far more likely to be of compelling interest to academe than other types of libraries. For instance, it is difficult for subject specialists to maintain contacts in parts of the war-torn Middle East. This inhibits the flow of information in parts of the world from which, arguably, we need information most.

Although the argument is rarely made, I hope that the crisis in scholarly communication and the shrinking of access caused by draconian intellectual property laws and the threats of special interests become increasingly identified as an issue of intellectual freedom. To date, the courts have been reluctant to make this argument.

Academic Libraries Need Policies

One of the first things a campus attorney asks in case of a controversial library action or complaint is, "What is your policy?" This book should convince you that, for all core activities in today's academic library, there is a need for a written policy. Collection policies demonstrate thoughtful consideration of how the library is spending ever-shrinking resources for a growing list of information requests. And in this era of national security concerns, libraries need to explain and justify their defense of freedom of expression. Library policies, goals, annual evaluations—all should be tied to the larger institutional mission. This includes all those "mom and apple pie" ideals about freedom of expression. One of the most important lessons I have learned in my thirty years in the profession is that there is no longer any consensus—even in what is considered to be the liberal world of academe—that the First Amendment as *applied* on campus is understood or supported. Senior administrators are likely to heed their attorneys and be overly cautious about pending legislation, or about contesting the meaning of "fair use."

Libraries need a well-documented purpose for every policy. A meeting room policy restricting the number of people in the room should state the reason for the restriction—the local fire code, for example. There also needs to be an appeal mechanism including due process—just as most campus grievance procedures already have. And the policies need to be an integral part of training and orientation for new staff. Academic librarians must take every opportunity to explain how the Library Bill of Rights applies to every dollar in the library budget and every activity and service the library promotes.

Websites with Policies and Updated Information

ACRL publications and documents:

- ACRL/AAUP/AAC "Joint Statement on Faculty Status of College and University Librarians" (1972), www.ala.org/ala/mgrps/divs/acrl/standards/jointstatementfaculty.cfm
- ACRL, "Faculty Status for College and University Librarians, Joint Statement and Standards" (2001), www.ala.org/ala/mgrps/divs/acrl/standards/standardsfaculty.cfm
- ACRL, "Academic Status for College and University Librarians" (January 2007), www.ala.org/ala/mgrps/divs/acrl/standards/guidelinesacademic.cfm
- ACRL Toolkit: "The Power of Personal Persuasion: Advancing the Academic Library Agenda from the Front Lines," www.ala.org/ala/mgrps/divs/acrl/issues/marketing/advocacy_toolkit.pdf
- ACRL, "Changing Roles of Academic and Research Libraries," from Round Table on Technology and Change in Academic Libraries, convened by ACRL, Chicago, November 2006, www.ala.org/ala/mgrps/divs/acrl/issues/future/changingroles.cfm
- AAUP, "1940 Statement of Principles on Academic Freedom and Tenure," www.aaup.org/AAUP/pubsres/policydocs/contents/1940statement.htm

Other valuable white papers and current legal news:

- Office for Intellectual Freedom of the American Library Association, "Intellectual Freedom Principles for Academic Libraries: An Interpretation of the Library Bill of Rights," in ALA, *Intellectual Freedom Manual*, 7th ed. (Chicago: American Library Association, 2006), 166–70.
- Scholarly Publishing and Academic Resources Coalition (SPARC), www.arl.org/sparc/. All information on this website is timely and valuable.

The Case of Ward Churchill

Ward LeRoy Churchill was a professor of ethnic studies at the University of Colorado at Boulder. He has written dozens of books and articles, mostly in the alternative press—his way of snubbing the academic mainstream peer review process. He has focused on several political issues for a general readership but especially on the history of Native Americans.

In 2005 he gained national notoriety for a September 12, 2001, essay—"Some People Push Back"—which he expanded for the compilation *On the Justice of Roosting Chickens: Reflections on the Consequences of U.S. Imperial Arrogance and Criminality.*

In that essay Churchill places some modicum of responsibility on the victims of the September 11 World Trade Center disaster, because they worked there as "technocrats" and "little Eichmanns," a reference to the banality of Adolf Eichmann's evil plans for the mass destruction of the Jewish people. In the same way, Churchill argues rather obliquely, the unwitting technocrats in the World Trade Center were victimizing the oppressed peoples of the world.[4]

Much of this came to light only after Hamilton College, New York, invited Churchill to speak in early 2005 as a guest of their Kirkland Project for Study of Gender, Society, and Culture. This presumably liberal-biased institute had already been under scrutiny by the American Council of Trustees and Alumni (ACTA) and by David Horowitz's Center for the Study of Popular Culture. Eventually, the Hamilton invitation and the Churchill essay hit the mainstream press.

Hamilton at first attempted to keep the date with Churchill, with a strong defense of academic freedom, but it later rescinded the invitation because of threats of campus violence.[5]

The contentious words from one of their tenured faculty members outraged many University of Colorado officials, but they initially defended Churchill's constitutional right to free speech. Ultimately, though, political pressure from the governor of Colorado and the national outcry led to a university investigation of Churchill's academic research by the Standing Committee on Research Misconduct. The committee found that Professor Churchill had plagiarized a significant amount of his writing, and on June 26, 2006, the University of Colorado announced its intent to dismiss Churchill. It did keep him on the payroll until the matter was finalized. Churchill filed an appeal, but in July 2007 the University of Colorado fired him for research misconduct.

In 2006, ACTA published the report "How Many Ward Churchills?" which demonstrates that Professor Churchill is not alone in his predicament. ACTA examined the websites of twenty-five top private colleges and universities plus the Big Ten and Big 12 institutions. It quotes course descriptions, syllabi, and faculty home pages to make the point that faculty are biased and trying to politicize students into one particular point of view.[6]

This controversy is important for librarians to ponder. Should a library collect Ward Churchill's books, which some assert are plagiarized or, at the very least, poor scholarship? Does an academic library remove them from the shelves after the fact?

What does a librarian do if a faculty member demands the removal of a book because it is not legitimate scholarly material? Does our library have a process or written policy on how to deal with this or similar situations? Does a librarian point a student to the Churchill essay on the Web? How do we know it is the authentic version, and should we care?

What academic constituencies (see the introduction to this book) would have an interest in a Ward Churchill controversy? What academic traditions come into play here? What policies should a library have in place to bolster its position? What role should librarians play when such a controversy affects their campus? What if the press interviews them? The Ward Churchill controversy, regardless of which side you come out on, has all the elements required for a healthy debate about intellectual freedom in library collections and services. See http://wardchurchill.net for a defense of Churchill's speech on grounds of academic freedom. ∎

CASE STUDY 2

Mahmoud Ahmadinejad Visits Columbia University

On September 24, 2007, Iranian president Mahmoud Ahmadinejad appeared in a World Leaders Forum event at Columbia University in New York City. President Lee Bollinger introduced him with an introduction many thought was not conducive to free speech. Bollinger, according to the *New York Times,* introduced him as a "cruel and petty dictator" and continued with a series of insults. Many in the audience were stunned at what they perceived as a lack of courtesy to academic guests; others thought Bollinger should not have invited him in the first place. The reaction from the Middle East was negative, especially because many academics in that region felt that basic rules of hospitality to a guest were violated.

When criticized by Columbia faculty, Bollinger replied that he was simply exercising his own rights of free speech.[7] *Time* magazine included Bollinger's introduction in their 2007 Top Ten Awkward Moments, which includes a video clip of Bollinger's introduction.[8] When interviewed by the university magazine *Columbia,* Bollinger defended his behavior:

> My role, as I saw it, was to introduce and help frame the Ahmadinejad appearance from my *own* perspective—and to give voice to my personal sense of intellectual objection and moral outrage—in order to set the stage for a serious debate about serious matters. The greatest danger is that we will not live up to our academic responsibilities to take ideas seriously. Questions and answers are very important, but sometimes we need more than that. . . . It is what I felt needed to be said, given the views and beliefs and actions that were on the table by virtue of the president of Iran's visit. Had I not expressed the full sense of opposition and challenge, I felt I would have let down the academic values at stake. I think part of being able to hold forums that address the most difficult and controversial issues is to be able to live with sharp exchanges that incorporate the passions, emotions, feelings, and beliefs that are directly challenged by the controversy of speakers.[9]

View the video clip, or if possible read a transcript of the event. Ahmadinejad's appearance at Columbia is a fascinating case study of academic freedom. Several issues come to play: traditional "rules of engagement" during academic forums; cultural differences; the difficult position of a college president when hosting a highly controversial public figure; the public relations considerations during campus controversies; and the role of alumni pressure in campus controversies. Bollinger has been praised in the past for numerous passionate defenses of academic freedom. Did this latest event promote that value? Are some campus speakers simply inappropriate, if they are likely to cause deep campus divides along ethnic, racial, or gender lines? ■

NOTES

1. Sam Demas, "From the Ashes of Alexandria: What's Happening in the College Library?" in *The Library as Place: Rethinking Roles, Rethinking Space* (Washington, D.C.: Council on Library and Information Resources, 2005), 28.
2. Geoffrey T. Freeman, "The Library as Place: Changes in Learning Patterns, Collections, Technology, and Use," in *Library as Place,* 3.
3. Patricia Cohen, "Spaces for Social Study," *New York Times,* August 1, 2004, Education Life, 19.
4. Ward Churchill, *On the Justice of Roosting Chickens: Reflections on the Consequences of U.S. Imperial Arrogance and Criminality* (Oakland, Calif.: AK Press, 2003). The essay is to be found in many forms on the Internet; the original, published online, can be found at www.darknightpress.org. For the "little Eichmanns" quotation, see, e.g., the AK Press edition, 19.
5. For Hamilton College's point of view, see www.hamilton.edu/news/wardchurchill/, an excellent place to get a full record of media coverage and Hamilton College's responses. Churchill's essay is also posted there.
6. This report is available for free downloading at www.goacta.org/publications/downloads/ChurchillFinal.pdf.
7. Tamar Lewin and Amanda Millner-Fairbanks, "President of Columbia Is Criticized," *New York Times,* November 14, 2007, Education section.
8. Elizabeth Salemme, "Top Ten Awkward Moments," *Time,* online edition, December 14, 2007, www.time.com/time/specials/2007/top10/article/0,30583,168204_168303_1690463,00.html.
9. Lee Bollinger, interviewed for "In the Eye of the Storm," *Columbia,* Fall 2007, 20.

CHAPTER 2

Collection Development

Lesson One: The bold act of reading. As noted in our Academic Plan, lux, libertas—light and liberty—are the founding principles of this University. We are ever mindful that knowledge is the guardian of liberty. . . . It is the university's responsibility to remain a vibrant intellectual community in which all viewpoints can be comfortably expressed and heard in an atmosphere of respect. Universities exist to promote the free exchange of ideas.

Robert N. Shelton, Executive Vice Chancellor and Provost,
University of North Carolina at Chapel Hill, Speech on March 17, 2005

The bold act of reading," from the epigraph above, is a cherished academic tradition kept alive by excellent campus library collections and access to information around the world. The library collection must be viewed as a university asset and investment, along with its art collection, campus facilities, distinguished faculty and librarians, and pool of students recruited in an increasingly competitive environment. Like other campus assets, traditional campus library collections require ongoing stewardship—

physical preservation, sometimes weeding, continual acquisition of new materials, cataloging for access, and, increasingly, provision of reference and instructional services to help users navigate the maze of resources.

Collection development best practices have changed dramatically since the last quarter of the twentieth century. Traditionally, collection development was focused on the expert selection of materials, printed on paper, to be cataloged, shelved, and circulated from a physical campus building. In the twenty-first century, collection development means the purchasing, borrowing, or licensing of access to information in a variety of formats from a variety of sources. Collections now include the following: bundled electronic serials purchased in consortia through a license; music on vinyl, CD, or via streaming services; books and journals in a regional joint storage facility and available through interlibrary loan; digitized student theses stored in the campus institutional repository; and a unique medieval manuscript available only by visiting one library's special collections department. Two current aphorisms certainly apply: "Libraries provide access, not just ownership," and "This library will make information available not 'just in case' but 'just in time.'"

A great deal of information in the twenty-first-century academic library has not been selected through traditional means. This includes open web content and electronic database content—and resources like Wikipedia. This new dynamic collection development environment calls for collection development librarians who can allocate ever-shrinking acquisitions budgets as prices rise and types of information resources increase and diversify. They must understand the publishing marketplace and new trends in scholarly communication. They must be able to negotiate licenses aggressively (including some demands that affect the intellectual freedom of users). They

Defending a Book: A Success Story at Clemson University

The successful and well-integrated campus library will always express its goals, activities, and financial needs in terms of the overall campus mission. Academic freedom is an example of a value that serves as common ground on most campuses. Many librarians, faculty, students, and administrators have demonstrated extraordinary courage, given these times: post–September 11 jitters, fear of not being granted tenure, and the increasingly short terms of high-level campus administrators because of the stress from alumni, faculty, and legislators.

I hope this and other examples throughout this book will inspire librarians—in both public and private institutions—because there are presidents and administrations that still hold dear the freedom to read.

Clemson University in South Carolina assigned, for its 2006 summer reading program for incoming freshman, the book *Truth and Beauty* by Ann Patchett. This campus is in a "red" state with a high percentage of conservative students, parents, and alumni, many of whom protested this assigned book because of its language and explicit manner. President James F. Barker was pressured by parents, elected officials, and presumably wealthy alumni to remove this book from the summer reading list. His response on the first page of the campus website is an inspiration to librarians who want to "hitch their intellectual freedom wagon" to the overall campus vision:

> Our response has been a strong defense of the principle that it is the responsibility of the university to determine what is taught and how it is taught. This is an academic assignment, the culmination of a faculty-driven selection process which I respect. In fact I am proud of the thoughtful way our faculty and staff made this selection. I have responded, in part, by writing that . . . students are required to read the book but they are not required to admire the characters. We never want our students to engage in unquestioning acceptance of anything they read, and the assignment does not mean Clemson endorses all the behavior recounted in the book. However, we believe it is incorrect and unfair to the author to characterize the book as "filth" or "pornography" based solely on excerpts quoted out of context. . . . I hope that a civil, intellectual discussion of the book, respectful of both the author and her critics, will be the outcome of this year's freshman reading experience for all.[1]

This statement could easily be used to defend library general collections, promote the importance of open and free inquiry, and underscore all the interpretations of the Library Bill of Rights.

need to develop collections for local campus curricular needs and, at the same time, decide which titles to purchase and which to access through interlibrary loan.

The art beyond the skill of collection development comes into play when librarians can envision the library's collections within the historic campus culture—the "institutional memory." Such librarians know the breadth and depth of collections, the peaks and valleys of collections funding over the years, and faculty research interests.

But most of all, true collection development professionalism embraces the principles of intellectual freedom in every decision to purchase or share library information resources. Librarians are prepared to make courageous decisions about controversial library materials. They are armed with written policies and professional principles for facing requests from powerful campus figures to remove books or block access to controversial content. They are able to articulate to an alumnus why he should continue his membership in the Library Friends despite his objection to the library's purchase of a rare collection of gay literature.

This new, diverse world of collections access is a blessing and a curse for advocates of intellectual freedom. Traditional book censorship challenges remain. In addition, the Internet has given rise to web content packaging that cannot be purchased piecemeal. Thus it is inevitable that some content is going to be offensive to some library users, and there is very little that librarians can do about it unless they cancel the entire package. Librarians no longer have the control they once had over content. On the other hand, this bundling of resources can be helpful when confronted by a student who objects to one abstract of one article within a database of thousands of abstracts. It is easy to say, "Just move on to another abstract; there are plenty of other choices."

The more likely problem for academic libraries is that some content will be deemed unscholarly and therefore inappropriate for academic research. The Internet has given rise to content from unknown sources, to sites with images truly illegal for minors to view, and to sites with undocumented "facts." The Internet has anointed all of us as potential authors—and that includes neo-Nazi groups with websites masked as legitimate sources for evidence about the Holocaust. Such material is convenient for students to access and use injudiciously, leading some professors to forbid students from footnoting *any* web content in their research papers. It is up to library information literacy programs to explain that some web content (e.g., electronic journal subscriptions) is just as authoritative as printed paper content and that the faculty should not "throw out the baby with the bath water." Currently, many campus librarians have agreed to teach an information literacy class, only to find that the faculty member wants the librarian to discourage the use of web content, when the students want to use nothing but!

Collection development of academic library content differs somewhat from that for public libraries. For example, the issue of scholarly worth and expertise often arises when deciding to purchase a title for the academic library. The excuse of "unscholarly" is often used to avoid purchase of controversial content. Recently one of my librarian colleagues was told by a faculty member, only somewhat jokingly, that academic libraries should purchase only books that contained footnotes.

SPECIAL COLLECTIONS

Academic institutions increasingly look to their library's special collections and archives to help provide a unique brand to the campus. The university archives can provide all sorts of photos and historic documents for everything from lawsuits to homecoming events. As reference and other collections become increasingly homogeneous, it is the unique collections that give each library its individuality. As campuses strive to give their students experience with primary resources as preparation for graduate school, more and more special collections units are opening their doors to undergraduates with information literacy programs and active outreach to the campus and outside community as well.

As special collections are increasingly used, they are becoming an integral part of the library's collections and services. But because they are unique, expensive, and often fragile, special collections require special handling. Their "special" nature may conflict with traditional intellectual freedom policies. There is, however, no reason that special collections materials and services cannot adhere to the basic principles of intellectual freedom. The ACRL Rare Book and Manuscripts Section has developed a series of policies for the security and longevity of special collections, but these can complement intellectual freedom policy in most aspects.

First and foremost, almost all major special collections departments in U.S. academic and research libraries have dramatically expanded their outreach services in the past two decades. They have opened their doors not only to advanced scholars but to undergraduates and even to K–12 school groups. This philosophy of increased and equitable access is a positive step toward demystifying these materials as much as possible without leaving them open to physical damage and theft.

Special collections are typically in closed stacks, but the motive is not to hide controversial materials from the public but to ensure that unique, fragile, and expensive materials survive for patrons in future decades. Motive is important and should be reflected in the collection development policies for the various collections. For example, it would be unacceptable for all gay materials in a library's collection to be kept in special collections.

Special collections libraries do keep circulation records for posterity, as a deterrence to theft. Often serial thieves visit a series of special collections libraries, and circulation records help trace these thefts. However, ALA policy recommends that such circulation records be kept in a secured place and be consulted only when absolutely necessary to trace a theft or missing item, page, illustration, or other part of a book.

Because of the nature of the retrieval process for materials in closed stacks, special collections librarians are often very aware of each user and what he or she is researching. It is the ethical obligation of special collections librarians to keep confidential the research topics and habits of their researchers, unless the researcher gives explicit permission for the librarian to tell someone else working on a similar topic and might want to collaborate or exchange ideas.

OVERARCHING PRINCIPLES OF INTELLECTUAL FREEDOM PERTAINING TO COLLECTION DEVELOPMENT AND MANAGEMENT

This book is based on the ethical values and principles of intellectual freedom as formulated and advocated by the leading U.S. library organizations. Many academic libraries have not adopted these principles. In fact, a great many institutions of higher education do not subscribe to them—often intentionally. Librarians should be aware of such differences among academic libraries and understand that especially in some private academic institutions the administration has more rights in regard to control over collection development in those institutions' libraries. Still, most prestigious

U.S. private academic institutions would not think of censoring content on campus, because they would have a difficult time recruiting the kind of faculty and students they want. And publicly funded academic institutions are subject to the pressure of state legislators, who are sometimes pressured by their constituencies to restrict what they view as liberally biased information in campus libraries. The important differences between private and public institutions are detailed in this book's introduction. For each of the principles below, librarians in private institutions should check with their legal counsel on applicability.

The following, brief list highlights important principles and recommendations drawn from ALA's Office for Intellectual Freedom, elaborated in the *Intellectual Freedom Manual,* 7th ed. (Chicago: American Library Association, 2006), and posted on the Office for Intellectual Freedom website (www.ala.org/oif/).

Code of Ethics of the American Library Association

II. We uphold the principles of intellectual freedom and resist all efforts to censor library resources.

Intellectual Freedom Manual, 244–45, or www.ala.org/ala/aboutala/offices/oif/statementspols/codeofethics/codeethics.cfm.

ALA Library Bill of Rights

Article II: Libraries should provide materials and information presenting all points of view on current and historical issues. Materials should not be proscribed or removed because of partisan or doctrinal disapproval.

Intellectual Freedom Manual, 55, www.ala.org/ala/aboutala/offices/oif/statementsols/
statementsif/librarybillrights.cfm.

Intellectual Freedom Principles for Academic Libraries: An Interpretation of the Library Bill of Rights

3. The development of library collections in support of an institution's instruction and research
programs should transcend the personal values of the selector. In the interests of research and
learning, it is essential that collections contain materials representing a variety of perspectives
on subjects that may be considered controversial.

Intellectual Freedom Manual, 166–68, or www.ala.org/ala/aboutala/offices/oif/statementspols/
statementsif/interpretations/intellectual.cfm.

Diversity in Collection Development: An Interpretation of the Library Bill of Rights

This excerpt incorporates the "access" model of providing content:

Librarians have a professional responsibility to be inclusive, not exclusive, in collection
development and in the provision of interlibrary loan. Access to all materials legally obtainable
should be assured to the user, and policies should not unjustly exclude materials even if they
are offensive to the librarian or the user.

Intellectual Freedom Manual, 117–18, or www.ala.org/ala/aboutala/offices/oif/statementspols/
statementsif/interpretations/diversitycollection.cfm.

Evaluating Library Collections: An Interpretation of the Library Bill of Rights

This interpretation offers guidance for weeding projects:

> This procedure is not to be used as a convenient means to remove materials presumed to be controversial or disapproved of by segments of the community.

Intellectual Freedom Manual, 136–37, or www.ala.org/ala/aboutala/offices/oif/statementspols/statementsif/interpretations/evaluatinglibrary.cfm.

Challenged Materials: An Interpretation of the Library Bill of Rights

> The American Library Association declares as a matter of firm principle that it is the responsibility of every library to have a clearly defined materials selection policy in written form which reflects the Library Bill of Rights, and which is approved by the appropriate governing authority. The Constitution requires a procedure designed to focus searchingly on challenged expression before it can be suppressed. An adversary hearing is part of this procedure. Therefore, any attempt, be it legal or extra-legal, to regulate or suppress materials in libraries must be closely scrutinized to the end that protected expression is not abridged.

Intellectual Freedom Manual, 111, or www.ala.org/ala/aboutala/offices/oif/statementspols/statementsif/interpretations/challengedmaterials.cfm.

Expurgation of Library Materials: An Interpretation of the Library Bill of Rights

> The act of expurgation has serious implications. It involves a determination that it is necessary to restrict access to the complete work. This is censorship. When a work is expurgated, under the assumption that certain portions of that work would be harmful

to minors, the situation is no less serious. . . . Further, expurgation without written permission from the holder of the copyright on the material may violate the copyright provision of the United States Code.

Intellectual Freedom Manual, 146–47, or www.ala.org/ala/aboutala/offices/oif/statementspols/statementsif/expurgatedlibrary.cfm.

Restricted Access to Library Materials: An Interpretation of the Library Bill of Rights

I place this interpretation in the collection development section of this book because so many academic libraries have distinguished special collections and archives divisions. Because of the cost, uniqueness, an often fragile condition of these materials, it is essential that they be housed separately in secure stacks. Some have asked whether this segregation of materials is a violation of the Library Bill of Rights. As this interpretation states, the key is intent:

> All proposals for restricted access collections should be carefully scrutinized to ensure that the purpose is not to suppress a viewpoint or to place a barrier between certain patrons and particular content. A primary goal of the library profession is to facilitate access to all points of view on current and historical issues.

Intellectual Freedom Manual, 197–98, or www.ala.org/ala/aboutala/offices/oif/statementspols/statementsif/interpretation/restrictedaccess.

A Dirty Book Is Seldom Dusty.

From a hand-printed poster by Amos Paul Kennedy Jr.

OTHER TOOLS

What kinds of intellectual freedom information should a collection development librarian have readily available? Following is a checklist:

Written collection development policies. All academic libraries should have locally created collection development policies to guide their selection decisions. Such policies not only help guide tough choices when money is tight, they also help librarians defend purchases challenged because of their content.

Written collection development policies from peer institutions. Such policies can help bolster your case if you are collecting graphic novels, for example, and faculty complain that these are not scholarly. If peer institutions are collecting graphic novels, this can help you argue that such material is of scholarly interest. Or, if peer institutions are not collecting them, you might argue that you are promoting diversity of information by collecting them on behalf of your peers or consortia or for interlibrary loan purposes. Consortia should be especially cognizant of member policies for purposes of resource sharing.

Campus student and faculty codes of conduct and guidebooks. The library should make sure that these and other campus codes reflect principles of library intellectual freedom. For example, no student's library privileges should be rescinded without access to a hearing with due process. Further, computer services and library services should have consistent policies about what constitutes misuse of library computer resources. *No library privileges should be rescinded over issues of content.* Copies of all policies should be close at hand in the library.

AAUP principles of academic freedom. The introduction to this book underscores the importance of principles of academic freedom as part of the library's advocacy of intellectual freedom on campus. The AAUP has been a loyal and longstanding ally of librarians' work and principles. See www.aaup.org.

Campus IT policies that may affect content access. All policies should be consistent with library policies, including those about confidentiality of student transactions, any filtering of content by the campus network, and procedures for USA PATRIOT Act inquiries. Librarians may well find unacceptable IT policies in place and should work with the appropriate managers to change them. Often these policies are developed by a campus technology committee with little thought to the impact on privacy or content regulation. Librarians are uniquely qualified to highlight these problems and make sure they get fixed.

Current state and federal statutes or guidelines on content, if any. There may be post–September 11 policies relating to government documents, for example, or "pornography" statutes that often allow research libraries and museums a different set of standards. Filtering bills should also be documented and monitored.

Current court cases relating to content, if any.

Campus speech code, if any. Many campus speech codes have been overturned in the courts. It is important to monitor such litigation. See the introduction for further information.

Public or private institution? This book's introduction explains differences that affect intellectual freedom practices in academic libraries. It is crucial that the library director understand the campus culture in regard to diversity of library collections. This information can be gleaned from written documents and past history (if any) of attempted censorship of library content—in any format, including the Internet.

Library procedure and staff training for handling requests and challenges regarding library content. These procedures should include responses to local challenges and other inquiries by law enforcement officials, including the FBI. Remember, too, that attempted censorship comes from the political left and right. Most book challenges on a campus are likely to be of a different kind than complaints about immorality or sexually explicit images. They are likely to be arguments that a particular work is too popular to spend money on, that it is offensive to women, that it is bad scholarship, and similar arguments.

A campus understanding that in most cases content, regardless of format, is treated the same in terms of principles of intellectual freedom. This understanding helps in situations in which Internet content is challenged but the very same content in a printed book is not.

Definitions of *pornography, obscenity,* and related terms. One of my major annoyances over the years has been the way these terms are tossed about, even among library professionals who should understand the distinctions. Proper use of these terms is important when law enforcement authorities or the courts are challenging particular library content. The distinctions are fuzzy, but it is important to discern them:

Pornography is not legal terminology; *child pornography* is (see below). And yet *pornography* is used indiscriminately by the media, lobbies and other pressure groups, and, yes, even in legislation from time to time. It is the kind of term that means one thing to one person and something else to another. It is also a very culturally bound term. One of the best accounts is the entry "Pornography and Censorship," in the online *Stanford Encyclopedia of Philosophy.* The author muses that there are three possible definitions—none of them legal terminology. One is that pornography is "sexually explicit material." The second is "sexually explicit material (verbal or pictorial) that is *primarily designed to produce arousal in viewers.*" The third is "sexually explicit material designed to produce sexual arousal in consumers *that is bad* in a certain way."[2]

Obscenity is a term of law, referring to speech that is "unprotected" by the First Amendment and may lead to criminal conviction if expressed. The Supreme Court has tried to define it many times, with minimal success. However, the standing definition derives from *Miller v. California* (413 U.S. 15 [1973]). There is a three-part test used in deliberations in a court of law (not by a librarian at a reference desk):

- Whether the "average person," applying contemporary community standards, would find that the work, taken as a whole, appeals to the prurient interest;
- Whether the work depicts or describes, in a patently offensive way, sexual conduct specifically defined by the applicable state law, and
- Whether the work, taken as a whole, lacks serious literary, artistic, political, or scientific value.[3]

Child pornography. In *New York v. Ferber* (458 U.S. 747 [1982]), the Supreme Court declared child pornography "a category of material outside the protection of the First Amendment." Child pornography is photographs or films depicting sexual activity by juveniles. The courts applied the *Miller* test above and added that, in the case of children, "a trier of fact need not find that the material appeals to the prurient interest of the average person; it is not required that sexual conduct portrayed be done so in a patently offensive manner; and the material at issue need not be considered as a whole."

If a librarian is faced with defining *harmful to minors* or *indecent,* he or she should contact a First Amendment attorney. These are terms of law, but the definitions and uses in court have been confusing.

"This book is blasphemous and doesn't reflect our institutional values and mission."

A young professor, newly tenured at a conservative Christian college, requests that the library purchase a theological treatise long rejected as heretical and blasphemous; he wants to assign the work to students in his philosophy classes. The chair of the theology department and the dean of the divinity school learn of the purchase and insist that the library remove the work, which they see as a threat to students' faith and belief. The school admits students without regard to their religious belief, and the faculty has adopted an academic freedom policy.

This case study could be applied to any situation in which a librarian is asked to purchase a controversial book. This particular situation is complicated by the fact that the library is part of a private religious college. Even so, the faculty has adopted an academic freedom policy, so it appears that the faculty value diversity of opinion.

This case study is not meant to single out Christian religious institutions. Librarians in private religious institutions of any denomination, or in any private institution wishing to impose a strong value system, could find themselves in this situation. Private institutions have a great deal of latitude in establishing parameters on the curriculum and on library content and services. While writing this case study I communicated with several librarians in theological seminaries and private religious colleges and universities. A great many of these libraries are in very liberal academic institutions, and many subscribe to the principles of academic freedom and the ALA Library Bill of Rights. I try to represent a diversity of opinion in the following responses.

Do Your Professional and Personal Values Fit Well within Your Institution?

In most cases, the librarian facing such dilemmas is already on the job and must make a decision. For those reading this case study while job hunting, let it serve as a red flag. It behooves librarian candidates for employment in private religious institutions—or in *any* institution, for that matter—to make sure they are personally and professionally comfortable with the institution's values. Such information can be gleaned from the institution's website and codes of conduct for students and faculty. The institution has every right to shape itself in whatever way it pleases, as long as it does not violate the community's civil rights or other applicable laws. Candidates should talk with faculty and peruse the course listings and library collections and collection development policy. Unless you are prepared to lead a revolution and accept the consequences, you may want to look elsewhere. And, if your religious beliefs are identical to the institution's, ask yourself if your religious beliefs trump library professional ethics, because sometimes dilemmas arise between the two.

Should Your Religious or Political Values Trump the Library Profession's Intellectual Freedom Values?

In a fascinating compilation, *Christian Librarianship: Essays on the Integration of Faith and Profession,* it is clear that not all librarians place professional ethics above their personal religious beliefs—but some do. As G. A. Smith puts it, "Love is the preeminent Christian virtue, a principle that can revolutionize the way librarians approach their work. Librarians' personal convictions take precedence over professional codes of ethics."[4] James R. Johnson's essay states:

> The concept of intellectual freedom promoted by the American Library Association is defective because of its basis in autonomous individualism; its relativistic approach to truth; its secular, anti-religious bias; its application to virtually all forms of expression; and its imposition as an ideology on all libraries. A distinctively Christian approach, emphasizing both individual and community rights, is proposed as a more satisfactory approach to intellectual freedom in the educational sphere of a pluralistic, democratic society.[5]

Another essay, by Donald Davis, is particularly valuable because he has worked in the secular library world (he taught collection development at the library school at the University of Texas at Austin) and is a self-professed evangelical Christian. Thus he serves as an interpreter between the world of the ALA's intellectual freedom values and the world of library associations for religious organizations. Davis calls for evangelicals to embrace intellectual freedom enthusiastically: "Bible college librarians should stimulate their campus communities to discuss controversial topics and engage in the integration of faith and life by collecting the best information resources—secular, broadly Christian, and evangelical." He urges librarians in all institutions to tie library collection development to the institutional mission. He argues that Bible colleges have a stated mission to provide education for Christian students *and* for work outside the institution. Therefore, a good understanding of faith and life outside the seminary argue for the inclusion of secular literature and ideas within the library:

> I confess that I have never understood why Bible colleges and institutes do not do more serious grappling with American popular culture—music, movies, television, best-selling books,

novels, and popular public issues. If you are training young people to enter contemporary society as light and salt, are you helping to prepare them to enter into meaningful friendships with neighbors and coworkers who are not steeped in evangelical culture? How will we ever be credible critics of our culture, and converse knowledgeably about the issues that occupy many people, unless we expose ourselves and our students to the ideas that concern our society?

Davis asks his audience: "On your campus are you simply an efficient administrator of a bibliographical warehouse, or are you an intellectual provocateur—an intellectual subversive—who is providing stimulus to all users?"[6]

Maybe We Should Use Closed Stacks to Solve the Problem

In yet another essay in the Davis and Smith volume, Roger W. Phillips tells the audience:

> In 1976 the Christian Librarians' Fellowship (now the Association of Christian Librarians [i.e., ACL]) held a workshop on censorship at its annual convention. The moderator distributed copies of *"Dirty Books" in Christian Schools: Principles of Selection.* The tone of the paper, rather than being censorious, is ameliorative. The basic plea of the paper is for Christian institutions to establish clearly defined selection policies that allow for the freedom of the writer and the freedom of the reader.
>
> Also distributed at that workshop was a reprint of an article on censorship and excerpts from Hebden Taylor's *The New Legality, in the Light of the Christian Philosophy of Law.* The article found little biblical precedent for censorship and concluded that Christians defend themselves from evil with the truth they have through faith in Jesus. Taylor's observations led him to a position of limited censorship. . . . No materials should be censored, but librarians can put materials in closed stacks.

Though these publications were distributed and discussed at the workshop, no conclusions were reached. The only clear statement was a call to each library to develop a written selection policy and that ACL draft a definition of censorship.[7]

Inspiration from the Trenches

These following e-mail responses to my e-mail query regarding this case study are included in the hope that they give librarians in this situation the optimism that they can prevail. All comments are from private libraries, where the school would be in its rights to remove the materials. Colleagues like these can provide necessary moral support during times of stress.

> I am a firm believer that the spectrum of the diversity of the church belongs in the library and we do our patrons and students a disservice if we ignore this principle—on either end of our traditions. So far the faculty is firmly on my side.—Library director at a theological seminary

> In addition to supporting the Mission Statement of the United Theological Seminary, and the aims and goals of theological education, the Library upholds and promotes the American Library Association's document on intellectual freedom.—From the mission statement of the United Theological Seminary of the Twin Cities, New Brighton, Minn.

> Our school is at the more liberal end of the theological spectrum, so I'm more apt to be challenged on collection resources that reflect very conservative viewpoints. Once I explain the role of a library, folks usually let it go. I've never been faced with a formal challenge.

> This case reminds me of an incident at a Catholic institution close by. The library had posters for the 'Great Minds Meet at the Library' series (Eleanor Roosevelt, ML King, Gandhi, and Margaret Sanger). The Sanger poster was a source of controversy and then mysteriously

disappeared from the library. The Library Director was adamant about reposting the missing poster, and it was done eventually.

We actually received only one challenge while I was a librarian at a religious college, and it was from a devout librarian on our staff. We stuck to our guns, because the book supported the curriculum, and the incident blew over.

What foolishness to think it would really matter. With the Internet, everything is more or less available whether or not we like it, so one book would hardly hold back the tide of a dissenting opinion.

Summary of the Case Study

Although ALA's statements on intellectual freedom probably conflict with any concept of "limited censorship," discussions of these types of issues are invaluable for any library organization. Often, as one is drafting policy or honing definitions, the conflicts within an association are clarified and can then be dealt with openly and some may even be resolved or compromises reached. Further, the ideas presented in response to this case study can be used in a variety of ways. For example, in a public library where local religious pressure groups call for books to be censored, there are plenty of arguments in *Christian Librarianship* from Christian evangelical librarians who oppose pulling books from the shelves or damaging them in any way.

On the best of days, personal religious or ethical beliefs and professional ethics match, but many times librarians are asked to defend a book they abhor—or to catalog a book with sexually explicit images that they feel are demeaning to women. A search committee cannot eliminate a candidate based on his or her views on intellectual freedom, but it should make its institutional stance clear so that the candidate can make an informed decision.

Now, let us assume that you work at an institution like that in the case study and face the order to remove a theological treatise from the shelves. First, you need to review the body of principles of intellectual freedom and tools presented in this chapter. The chances of being able to defend the purchase of this book appear to be good, since the institutional values do include a statement on academic freedom and students are admitted regardless of their personal views. The fact that this is a private institution means that you must rely heavily on local institutional values of academic freedom, plus library professional ethics, to bolster your argument.

Second, you can use these tools to ascertain your campus's cultural values in regard to intellectual freedom. The fact that your institution has adopted principles of academic freedom, for example, should help you retain the book. Also, if students are admitted regardless of their religious faith, and there is no required declaration of belief on the part of students or faculty, you have further ammunition to defend the library as part of the stated campus mission to uphold academic freedom and to accommodate a diversity of religious beliefs. You should try to get support or advice from the American Theological Library Association or other library associations of your peer institutions. Also, the essays in *Christian Librarianship* or similar statements from colleagues in peer institutions may help.

Is your library chartered as a research institution? If it is, then the library has an obligation to retain a depth and breadth of materials, even those that are not in the curriculum or are currently out of style.

When you speak with the dean or your boss in your attempt to keep the book on the shelves, point out that students will probably be able to find it on the Internet anyway. If they are creative enough they will look at OCLC's WorldCat or another resource and find it somehow. You might argue that it is better to buy an authoritative, perhaps annotated, edition for the campus, so students can discuss it with the professor and the librarians can help them find similar books on the same topic from a variety of points of view. This line of argument for promoting a pedagogy of critical thinking may be persuasive.

Sometimes academic administrators are repelled by highly ideological arguments. You might decide it would be better strategy to work with the faculty member to write up a justification of the purchase in terms of how this book supports the curriculum. It might include assurances that this book will be taught within the context of other treatises with other points of view. You could also offer an information literacy class to support the course and present other library resources available to the students.

In this case you are fortunate that the faculty member is tenured; otherwise, you need to be very sensitive to his or her difficult political position.

If your library has a written collection development policy, congratulations! It is important that libraries have such policies, written with the help of faculty. Academic libraries have widely varying missions. Research libraries have more depth and breadth in their collections and are likely to have controversial or currently unfashionable materials. They are less likely to deaccession outdated materials. On the other hand, non-research libraries may adhere more closely to curricular needs. No library can buy everything, so interlibrary loan must be considered a part of any collection development strategy in any institution. If one is in a consortium and is expected to purchase certain materials in support of that arrangement, it may be difficult to self-censor based on doctrinal objections. ∎

CASE STUDY 2

"These books are scholarly trash."

Lest librarians in nonreligious institutions think that secular academic libraries are protected from book challenges, here's an example that proves otherwise. A controversy over *Black Athena* was featured on the cover of the *Chronicle of Higher Education* (October 5, 2001), and many librarians were pressured not to buy this book. Below are examples of materials that have been censored (sometimes with little success) in academic libraries—materials that you may well be called upon to defend. Other categories might be content offensive to women or other protected classes and information that might arouse hate or offend certain groups.

Holocaust Denial Literature

Holocaust denial literature is problematic in academic libraries, not only because of the pain it causes to so many members of the Jewish and other directly affected communities but also because this literature is considered by the vast majority of scholars worldwide to be bogus and therefore unworthy to be on the shelves of an academic library. Further, many countries prohibit Holocaust denial literature on library shelves, so there are barriers to international interlibrary loan strategies. The *Encyclopaedia Judaica* provides an excellent outline of the issue, with key publications, websites, and personalities.[8]

Librarians in U.S. research institutions usually have holdings of the major Holocaust denial literature so that scholars can study the controversy. A brief look at OCLC's WorldCat database shows that many major U.S. universities, including the Jewish Theological Seminary, do have some titles. Some libraries use interlibrary loan for patron requests and thus avoid controversy over a purchase. The problem with this strategy is that it places pressure on those few libraries that own the title. Presumably, regardless of how insulting this literature is to scholars, most want it to survive if for no other reason than to serve as a historic example. See the following case study, on *Protocols of the Elders of Zion,* which presents some of these same issues for collection development in academic libraries.

Wikipedia

In 2006, Middlebury College's department of history approved a policy that students not cite Wikipedia in their research papers.[9] Wikipedia has become a lightning rod in academe for those who view "peer review" and "expertise" as outdated elitist notions, in contrast to those who think that authentication and documentation are on the decline and that scholarship is suffering as a result. Librarians should understand how Wikipedia is created, in contrast to peer-reviewed publications, so that they can present both types of resources to students in information literacy sessions.

My institution has taken what I believe is a wise approach. Wikipedia is presented in information literacy sessions as one of many types of information. Students learn how entries are created, critiqued, edited, and monitored. They are told that the content is fluid and thus that a citation in a dissertation, for example, may not be valid years from now. For getting basic information to start a project, though, Wikipedia may be just fine.

Wesleyan's approach echoes the attitude of Peter J. M. Nicholson's recent article in the *Chronicle of Higher Education*. An information literacy module for Wikipedia might look something like this:

> Define the problem for the students: What constitutes "intellectual authority" in academe today. Nicholson states: "People are much less prepared to defer to the acknowledged experts in various fields. At the same, time, however, we are being swamped with data and information—a glut that cries out for analysis and summary."[10] He suggests that Wikipedia is a great "first cut" at information. He believes that we need to classify information within an "ecosystem" where different types of information can be defined and used for different purposes.
>
> Help in what Nicholson calls "discovery and classification" of various types of information. We need to become "sophisticated consumers" of information and understand how each type is created.
>
> Distinguish Wikipedia from the more traditional peer-reviewed journals. A great assignment is for a student to trace the history and evolution of a particular journal. Many titles have not only a traditional print or electronic version but also blogs and wikis as supplements and added material on the website.

Controversial Works by Controversial Faculty

See "The Case of Ward Churchill" in chapter 1.

Pseudoscience

Science libraries are sometimes challenged if they purchase materials that diverge from the scientific method or are based on trends not yet substantiated by well-conducted research. Examples include books for and against global warming and books on intelligent design. There are, however, some defenses built into scientific publications. For one, scholars and inexperienced students alike are somewhat protected from bogus scientific theories by the citation system; major citation indexes include only those publications that are deemed by an editorial board to be worthy of inclusion. Second, syllabi and information literacy sessions can point out those writings and scientists who are distinguished in their fields.

At Wesleyan's Science Library, at a very liberal institution, a student came up to the science librarian surprised that we would have a book denying that global warming exists. Our librarian used this as a teachable moment about differing points of view. This is why I am such a supporter of information literacy as a way to keep collections diverse and teach students how to discern among resources.

A related issue arises when scientific information is no longer valid. For example, what about books about gay sex that were written before the AIDS epidemic and thus do not promote safe sex? This problem illustrates the need for written collection policies. A research library would arguably collect all books about gay sex for the historical record. For an undergraduate liberal arts college library, one might argue that only the most current editions are necessary. For colleges with curricular strengths in human sexuality, one would argue that all editions should be available.

Books in Controversial Areas of Scholarship

One of the most fascinating issues in academic library collection development is that of purchasing collections for new curricular interests. One highly publicized case was the controversy over *Black Athena: The Afroasiatic Roots of Classical Civilization* by Martin Bernal. The three volumes were published from 1987 to 2006 by Rutgers University Press and others. Bernal posited a new theory about the origins of Greek civilization, focused on Afrocentric contributions. In so doing, he also attacked the previous theories, which he believed were tainted by racism. Within academe this work created a furor and much published criticism from a variety of points of view. Bernal was criticized for being far too speculative and using linguistics as his only evidence. I know at least one librarian who was pressured not to buy these volumes, despite the fact that Bernal and others were on the lecture circuit and at least some in the academic community wanted to read the work before critiquing it.

A similar uproar occurred over *Time on the Cross: The Economics of American Negro Slavery* by Robert Fogel and Stanley Engerman, who argued that slaves actually lived better than factory workers in the industrial North, using plantation records and economic indicators as evidence. Both authors were accused of being apologists for slavery when in fact they both opposed it on moral grounds.

In the case of a controversial book, the best approach is to buy it. If it is extremely controversial, it can be the centerpiece for an exhibition including books offering other points of view or the focus of a program with a faculty panel discussing the book from various perspectives. Rather than hide the purchase, it is sometimes far better to publicize it within a broader context, so that the community knows that the library offers a diversity of views in its collections.

Popular Literature

When acquisitions budgets are tight, library purchases are sometimes scrutinized by faculty to make sure that no money is wasted on "popular" materials. This situation has arisen in regard to best sellers, computer games, manga, comic books, Hollywood blockbuster DVDs, and CDs of popular music.

Many academic libraries do indeed depend on their local public libraries to buy mystery novels and other popular works. It is not so easy, though, when universities offer majors in computer game theory and design. Also, a Japanese film course could easily refer to the influence of manga literature, which would then become an appropriate purchase for an academic library. Williams College Library now sponsors computer game nights weekly. Academic libraries are eager to be lively, heavily populated social spaces as well as sites for hard-core research. Some are willing to indulge some acquisitions funds, if necessary, to help create that atmosphere.

Again, a written collections policy is of immense help in these types of situations.

Pornography, Obscenity, and Child Pornography

Earlier in this chapter *pornography, obscenity,* and *child pornography* are defined. There are important distinctions, particularly when a library is attacked or approached by law enforcement officers for making "porn" available in the library. The important thing to remember, particularly in the case of alleged pornography, is that, legally, library content is protected by the First Amendment *regardless of its format, in most cases*. That means that in an academic library of adult users it is equally legal to view a Robert Mapplethorpe photograph in a printed art book sitting on a library table and to view it on a computer screen. Recently, many academic librarians have reported of patrons complaining about other patrons viewing pornography at neighboring terminals. Chapter 3 provides sample policies and suggested responses to such situations.

Academic libraries are often in a quandary, because freshmen are often under the age of twenty-one and some obscenity laws apply to minors. Legislation has usually been written to focus on the protection of younger minors. To date, no case has been brought against an academic library for providing access to a minor for illegal materials.

A related problem sometimes arises on college campuses when advocacy groups target library collections as a cause for oppression. For example, in the 1980s legal activist Catherine MacKinnon lodged an all-out attack on pornography as a violation of women's civil rights. Depictions of women in sexually explicit situations often places them in a subservient role, and thus MacKinnon argued that pornography contributes to the continuing oppression of women.[11]

Information That Promotes Terrorism

After September 11, the Federal Document Depository system required that depository libraries destroy or return print and multimedia documents to the government. They also removed from some government website information deemed sensitive. Some libraries have been attacked for buying the writings of Osama Bin Laden, even as scholars have been urging their students to read the words of terrorists in order to understand their motives. As with any kind of controversial topic, the library would do well to buy such material and surround it with a diversity of points of view.

Internet Content, including Social Software

Social networking is an important part of the lives of most undergraduates. This includes text messaging, wikis, blogs, podcasts, Facebook postings, and other Web 2.0 applications. Content comes to students through these means, so academic libraries must provide spaces and means for students to use these tools for obtaining content. There is also content created on campus and stored in institutional repositories. Collection development policies must cover this kind of content.

What Is a Librarian to Do? A Summary of Case Study 2

It must be clear by now that a written collection development policy is essential, not only as a planning and budget document but as a means to justify all purchases. Once this document has been approved by the appropriate campus officials, the library should purchase materials and access to materials according to the specifications and priorities laid out in the collection development document.

Academic libraries, like all libraries, make collections decisions based on a limited budget. Books that one expects to be used heavily or to be placed on course reserve should be purchased for the permanent collection. Books requested by faculty and students are often given special consideration. These requests should be filled as much as possible. Fiscal limitations can lead to cancellation of less used materials, and this can reduce access to lesser known authors, ideas, and publishers. Collections librarians should factor this threat of the shrinkage of diversity of views into their planning and into their relationships with consortia.

Minors and the University Library

Legal minors (those under the age of eighteen) use university and college libraries in increasing numbers. These minors may be full-time students, participants in a high school's college bridge program, or simply members of the public who take advantage of the rich resources in the university library at the invitation of the university.

Minor users in the university library raise questions concerning the library's responsibility for those users. Laws like the Children's Internet Protection Act (CIPA) require public schools and public libraries receiving certain federal funding to install filters on library computers in order to prevent youth under seventeen from accessing Internet materials deemed obscene or "harmful to minors." Is the university library obliged to exercise similar care for its minor users?

The answer, in general, is no. Although courts have recognized a limited duty on the part of universities to secure the physical safety of students in the wake of several tragedies resulting from hazing and underage drinking, no court has imposed a duty on university libraries to supervise the intellectual activities of legal minors who are students or are using the library for research and study. Modern law provides that colleges and universities are not ordinarily *in loco parentis* with their students, and the custodial and tutelary responsibilities of the elementary and high school do not apply. Students who are legal minors thus generally enjoy the same educational rights and privileges as their older colleagues.[12]

In addition, laws that might otherwise impose a duty on universities and university libraries to prevent the distribution of obscene or "harmful to minors" materials to minors customarily do not apply to institutions of higher education, in deference to their unique educational mission.[13]

To date, only one court has addressed the liability of a library for providing Internet access to minors who are subsequently exposed to sexually explicit content. In *Kathleen R. v. the City of Livermore,* the California Court of Appeals held that the mother of a twelve-year-old boy who used a library computer to view and download sexually explicit images published on the Internet could not sue the local public library for failing to prevent her child from accessing such materials.

The court dismissed the mother's lawsuit because the Communications Decency Act provides legal immunity to Internet service providers who merely provide access to Internet materials published or posted by third parties. The court also ruled that the library had no constitutional duty to protect minor children from harmful materials on the Internet, since the library did not have a custodial or other special relationship with its minor users. The court specifically rejected the mother's claim that the library intentionally exhibited obscenity or material harmful to minors by allowing minors to use their computers, on the grounds that the claim was inconsistent with library policy stating that library computers were to be used only for "educational, informational and recreational purposes" and prohibiting the use of computer resources for illegal purposes.

As illustrated by the California court opinion, well-crafted Internet use policies are an important tool for university and college libraries serving minors who are not students and who may be much younger than the university's student population. Such policies should outline the library's mission and guidelines for Internet use, prohibit use of computer facilities for illegal purposes, and inform parents who allow their children to use the university library that the parents, and not library employees, are responsible for monitoring their children's Internet activity.

Additional Resources

Communications Decency Act, 47 U.S.C. § 230
Freeman v. Busch, 349 F.3d 582 (10th Cir. 1993)
    (*in loco parentis* doctrine)
Kathleen R. v. City of Livermore, 87 Cal. App. 4th 684
    (Cal. Ct. App. 2001)

Subject selectors in an academic institution often select scholarly works simply because they are what students and faculty need. Other more popular works, if not in the collection statement, can be borrowed, often from public libraries. As we move increasingly into an environment of consortia, we should try to balance the permanent collection so that a variety of points of view are still represented—even when much needs to be borrowed. Because of the new environment, when collections are virtual as well as owned and physically on local shelves, librarians should strive for balance. That means that interlibrary loan must work well—that access must be assured and arranged for those materials that cannot be bought locally. Interlibrary loan should be used not to avoid politically difficult purchase decisions but to supplement local collections. In order to be a borrower, a library should be a good lender too. ■

CASE STUDY 3

Would You Buy This Book? Where Would You House It?

Should an academic library have books that are "fakes"? That espouse ethnic or racial hatred? If you buy it, should it be classified with other books that are not "fake"?

The Protocols of the Elders of Zion is an anti-Semitic tract published in Russia in 1905. It is probably a compilation of several anti-Semitic literary texts or pamphlets of the time, with boilerplate stereotypes of Jews plotting to conquer the world. The "protocols" are supposedly a list of twenty-four methods Jews can use to take over the world. The Jewish elders in the tract are teaching a new elder these tricks. Examples of protocols include using foreign loans to force national bankruptcy, advocating a world government, and introducing such revolutionary ideas as Darwinism and Marxism.

Scholarly consensus is that the Russian secret police created this text, which reflected the sentiments of those who opposed the Russian revolutionary movement. This book was exposed as a literary hoax as early as the 1920s but lives on whenever anti-Semitism arises. The book is still in print, and in fact there is a recent "Knight without a Horse," broadcast in the Arab world, based on it. It is quoted as factual in some textbooks in Middle Eastern countries.

Right before his death, Will Eisner, a cartoonist and graphic novelist, turned his talents to this famous book. Instead of writing a scholarly tome about the book's impact, Eisner decided to do a graphic novel, accessible to a popular audience. His book shows how a British reporter unravels the text and determines it is a hoax, then publishes that fact in the *Times* of London in 1921. It has an introduction by novelist Umberto Eco and gets academic imprimatur with an afterword by Steven Bronner, professor of political science at Rutgers University. Its extensive bibliography, including websites, is a great way to teach or learn about how a piece of propaganda becomes known in some cultures as a historical account.[14]

Librarians and faculty could use this book to demonstrate to students how anti-Semitism or other ethnic stereotypes get started. It could be used in the debate about Wikipedia and the importance of careful documentation. It should also be noted that a perusal of the library catalog at the Jewish Theological Seminary shows that the *Protocols* is on its shelves—a testament to the idea that to learn about anti-Semitism one needs to have access to those who promote it.

Amazon.com had a problem with the book, which it sells. According to the website, a rumor started that Amazon.com had favorably reviewed the book. This, the website states, is an "urban legend." It does sell the book, and it defends the decision:

> *The Protocols of the Learned Elders of Zion* is classified under "controversial knowledge" in our store, along with books about UFO's, demonic possession, and all manner of conspiracy theories. . . . As a bookseller, Amazon.com strongly believes that providing open access to written speech, no matter how hateful or ugly, is one of the most important things we do. It's a service that the United States Constitution protects, and one that follows a long tradition of booksellers serving as guardians of free expression in our society.
>
> Not all countries view these issues the same way. And one of our greatest challenges is to work cooperatively with other governments to respect their laws without compromising our core values of free expression and free exchange of information—values that the Internet embodies on a global scale.

This point alludes to the fact that some Western European countries forbid the sale of anti-Semitic materials.

The question for academic libraries is whether to buy this book or not. It is believed by most scholars to be a literary hoax, so how is it classified? Is it placed on the shelves or in special collections? Should academic libraries buy books that are hoaxes? Do they label them or house them as such?

A quick survey of the Web suggests that the Jewish Theological Seminary holds what appear to be all editions of this work, including some pamphlets. One supposes that they are collecting it as examples. The same is true of the Anti-Defamation League. These acquisitions would be consistent with the idea that one needs to understand the nature of the hatred in order to combat it. Many libraries, including that at the Jewish Theological Seminary, appear to keep copies in their special collections department. This is often done for books that are likely to be stolen or defaced, and sometimes for those that are offensive. Academic librarians need to consider how they are going to house such controversial books. ■

NOTES

1. James F. Barker, originally posted on the Clemson University website; contact Clemson University archives. The entire incident is recounted in an interview with Patchett; see Abigail Cutler, "My Pornography," *Atlantic,* July 16, 2007, www.theatlantic.com/doc/200707u/ann-patchett.
2. Caroline West, "Pornography and Censorship," *Stanford Encyclopedia of Philosophy* (http://plato.stanford.edu), first published May 5, 2004, 2.
3. Judith Silver, "Movie Day at the Supreme Court of 'I Know It When I See It': A History of the Definition of Obscenity," Findlaw, http://library.findlaw.com/2003/May/15/132747.html.
4. Gregory A. Smith, "A Rationale for Integrating Christian Faith and Librarianship," in *Christian Librarianship: Essays on the Integration of Faith and Profession,* ed. Gregory A. Smith (Jefferson, N.C.: McFarland, 2002), 17.
5. James R. Johnson, "A Christian Approach to Intellectual Freedom in Libraries," in *Christian Librarianship,* 139.
6. Donald G. Davis Jr., "Intellectual Freedom and Evangelical Faith," in *Christian Librarianship,* 131, 136–37.
7. Roger W. Phillips, "Library Encounters Culture," in *Christian Librarianship,* 94.
8. *Encyclopaedia Judaica,* "Holocaust Denial," www.encyclopaediajudaica.com.
9. *Chronicle of Higher Education,* May 21, 2006, 6.
10. Peter J. M. Nicholson, "The Intellectual in the Infosphere," *Chronicle of Higher Education,* March 9, 2007, B6.
11. Catherine MacKinnon, *Toward a Feminist Theory of the State* (Cambridge, Mass.: Harvard University Press, 1991).

12. For example, the Family Educational Rights and Privacy Act (FERPA) grants parents the right to examine their child's school records until the child turns eighteen. When a legal minor enrolls in a college program, the parents' FERPA rights terminate and pass to the student, even though the student may not become a legal adult for months or even years.
13. State laws addressing the distribution of materials deemed obscene or "harmful to minors" are not uniform and work differently in each state. Legal counsel should be consulted concerning the applicability of these laws to the university and the university library when drafting library policy.
14. Will Eisner, *The Plot: The Secret Story of the Protocols of the Elders of Zion* (New York: W. W. Norton, 2005).

CHAPTER 3

Internet Access

[The Internet] . . . constitutes a vast platform from which to address and hear from a world-wide audience of millions of readers, viewers, researchers, and buyers. . . . any person with a phone line can become a town crier with a voice that resonates farther than it could from any soapbox.

Reno v. ACLU (1997)

Streams of light versus ink on paper. This is the main change I have been concerned with and with which the law is being challenged. Our books are both a tool and a symbol—something to read and use, something to hold up and display, something to represent our goals and ideas. Paper? Discrete, boundaried, fixed, authoritative, trustworthy. And light? Powerful, stimulating, shifting, spreading, exposing, expanding, animating, unifying. . . . Who is holding the light? Who is hiding behind it? Does it shine on us all? How can we use it? How long will it last? Is this, indeed, a light without shadows, without boundaries, without a surrounding field of darkness?

M. Ethan Katsch, *Law in a Digital World*

These two epigraphs highlight two major themes affecting the Internet in libraries. First, the Supreme Court declared the Internet to be a powerful conduit for free speech and accurately prophesied its potential as a medium for democratic communications. Second, legal scholars have been wondering if the same free speech and intellectual property laws can actually be applied effectively to the unique characteristics of Internet speech. These two aspects of the Internet—its democratic potential and its unique qualities for providing access and carrying content—will be analyzed for decades to come.

THE INTERNET IN HIGHER EDUCATION

All U.S. academic institutions, including libraries, depend on the Internet not only for content but for software applications, handheld devices, Web 2.0, Blackboard and other courseware, distance learning—it is an endless and ever-growing list. Typical college students use a web-based portfolio to keep track of courses, grades, and progress toward graduation. They depend on course management software for course readings and communications among faculty and classmates. They access blogs, wikis, and RSS feeds on their library website. And, of course, social networking technologies such as MySpace add another level of complexity to their personal communications strategy. Students incorporate film clips into research "papers." The Internet sometimes replaces traditional library functions—electronic reserves is an example—but also adds new genres (games) and communications strategies unknown a decade ago. Williams College Library hosts a weekly computer game night. This would have been unheard of ten years ago.

Faculty also use the Internet to enhance pedagogy. At my institution one faculty member creates a website for her faculty summer institute in Jewish studies, with text of all the lectures and discussions and linked references to the readings, so that students can interact with the site during the following academic year to see how graduate seminars among colleagues are conducted. Another professor has created a social psychology network, which supports international communication among colleagues as well as the posting of important news and job openings in the profession. Another faculty member has created a "learning object," a computer-generated presentation of the evolution of a chick embryo. It can be downloaded for worldwide use.

THE INTERNET IN ACADEMIC LIBRARIES

How have the Internet and the Web changed academic library collections and services? The academic library landscape has been totally transformed.

The Internet provides access to materials formerly published on paper but now delivered to the desktop. The Web is an ideal platform for reformatting, displaying, and delivering traditional print content. The Internet also provides the platform for institutional repositories, which empower local faculty and students to store scholarly drafts, theses, and other research in a globally accessible repository rather than in cardboard archival boxes.

Thus the Internet is more than the "Wild West"; it also holds traditional but reformatted content, some of which is available only on the Internet. Librarians sometimes need to clarify this with more traditional faculty who still believe that Internet content should not be cited in papers. In contrast are their students, some of whom never use anything *but* Internet content in their research. A librarian committed to intellectual freedom teaches information literacy classes that discuss the types of materials available in all formats, with the features of each title or type, in order to promote diversity of information resources.

Librarians must also make library users and administration aware that they will treat Internet content in the same way as content on paper when it comes to issues of intellectual freedom—with obvious exceptions. Most libraries would not buy published, printed child pornography, which is illegal to possess, unless it were a library like the Kinsey Institute, which collects sexually explicit materials as an integral part of its educational mission. And yet a library user on any unfiltered terminal (and even on a filtered terminal) might inadvertently discover such material on the Internet. On the other hand, a Mapplethorpe photo on the Internet and in a traditional art book are both afforded First Amendment protection, and both might well be available in an academic library.

The Internet also supports the creation of new types of content. Wikipedia is one good example. It is a constantly changing encyclopedia that does not rely on traditional academic fact checking or on what some assert to be an elitist cabal of academic specialists. As a result, many faculty and scholars reject Wikipedia as nonscholarly. Any information resource that becomes labeled in that way is then discouraged as a source for a serious research paper. The role of a good information literacy program is to explain how Wikipedia works and how students and faculty might use it rather than ban or filter it (see chapter 2). Students need to be exposed to a variety of information resources so that they can learn for themselves how to sort out the biases and features of each.

The Internet has created all sorts of copyright dilemmas that are still being discussed as new formats continually emerge. Intellectual property law (not a focus in this book) has the potential to choke access to new kinds of Internet content, and so the First Amendment and copyright concerns are colliding more often than ever before. Librarians must keep current with intellectual property legislation and government policies because of this uneasy balancing act between providing access to information users and protecting the rights of those who create that information in the first place—and on whom libraries depend for information content.

The Internet viewed on a library reading room screen can be an "in your face" medium. What is being viewed by one user can sometimes be seen by the neighboring user—and by the librarian on duty. Librarians are more likely to become aware of what a user is viewing at a workstation than what a user is reading at a table. All kinds of anxiety and uncertainty arise when a librarian happens to glance at content he or she believes may be illegal. Neighboring users may also be offended by someone's content viewing choices. Privacy is easily compromised in the workstation environment.

Librarians have a variety of strategies to address this situation. Privacy screens are one ideal solution, so that users can view resources in relative privacy with minimal impact on adjacent users. Another solution is to place terminals in a variety of spaces. Some might be placed near a reference desk, others more remote. Catalogs and vendors can show how furniture can alleviate privacy concerns.

Internet content cannot be easily controlled or mediated. Traditional collection development applies to the Internet only for those traditional materials reformatted onto the Web or for those websites the library selects and highlights on the library website. In the case of open Internet content, it is likely that even with filters users occasionally discover obscenity (illegal) by accident. And undoubtedly the Internet surfer will encounter content that is legal but offensive to some.

The Internet is a communications device as well as a content container. Therefore, e-mail correspondence suspected of linkage to terrorists or sexual predators can lead to hard drives being confiscated by law enforcement officials. Open-access public terminals cause post–September 11 concern, for libraries cannot afford to be held liable for anonymous patrons' e-mail activity. The current Communications Assistance for Law Enforcement Act (CALEA) implementation and other legislation and court cases have the potential to chill Internet access in academic libraries (see chapter 5).

Finally, Internet content and communications can be filtered. U.S. academic libraries do not normally filter content, because of the strong culture of academic freedom in higher education and because these institutions compete to attract the best scholars, who demand unfettered access for research. And yet most colleges and universities now host a variety of programs for high school students and young adults—not to mention that undergraduates seem to be getting younger every year. At some point there may emerge enough of a critical mass of these "older minors" to make some colleges and universities rethink their commitment to unfiltered access. Thus far, however, state legislators have focused on protecting young minors and been willing to create exceptions for higher education when drafting state obscenity legislation.

One cold comfort is that filters are still not effective. The second edition of a report from the Brennan Center for Justice at New York University's School of Law concludes that filters are still incapable of discerning content as advertised. The 2001 first edition of the report reviewed nineteen filters and found that, even with improvements, they still overblock. In 2004 the second edition reports that filters still

> deprive users of many thousands of valuable web pages, on subjects ranging from war and genocide to sex and public health. . . . the widespread use of filters presents a serious threat to our most fundamental free expression values. . . . Filters provide a false sense of security, while blocking large amounts of important information in an often irrational or biased way.[1]

This book on academic libraries does not devote much time to the topic of filters, but the ALA website maintains current information on that issue. I have not found evidence of filtering controversies in U.S. academic libraries, though it remains a difficult international problem for academic libraries in authoritarian regimes.

THE ACADEMIC LIBRARY AND THE INFORMATION TECHNOLOGY DEPARTMENT

On most campuses the library and IT department are separate and often operate with different priorities and goals. In my experience the difference in approach, when it comes to the *rights of users,* is one of the most overlooked factors in successful collaboration between the two operations, and campus administrations ignore it at their peril. IT operations are far more likely to focus on user *responsibilities.* For example, if a student is suspected of downloading music and the recording industry has threatened the campus or that student with a lawsuit, the IT response might be to restrict access to the campus network before affording that student his or her due process rights—which are usually outlined in the campus student handbook. Being blocked from the campus network means being blocked from use of much of the library's resources. This right to access to information is, arguably, a constitutional guarantee, at least in a public institution.

The differences between the two approaches to Internet access can also be divisive in the area of privacy. It is essential that a librarian be at the table when campus administrators determine policies in the areas outlined below. Many IT activities are about the important issues of installation, response time, connectivity, network security, and the cost-efficient use of campus resources. But there are other issues surrounding user access and convenience on the service delivery point. The recent CALEA rulings are a case in point. In late 2008 the rulings in regard to libraries are still unclear. One campus might require authentication at every terminal in its library and another might not—even when the situation at each campus is identical. Attorneys have simply interpreted the FCC rulings and assessed the campus risk differently. When librarians were at the table during campus CALEA decision making, privacy concerns often prevailed.

Many campuses simply took the easy way out and locked their terminals down, even if the legal interpretations and FCC regulations were not yet set down. There have been resultant problems with lack of access for campus alumni, conference attendees, community groups, and users of government documents (if the library is a federal depository library, then public access to web-based documents is required by law).

Here are some questions that the campus library and IT department should discuss before a crisis arises:

- Is there a privacy policy in place for campus IT activities? Are privacy features an important aspect of investigating or negotiating for new products?
- What are the long-term strategies of the IT department? Library goals tend to have a longer time line; IT activities tend to be more project-based with shorter time lines. This difference in operation is something to be aware of in library/IT collaborations.
- Is any content filtered or blocked from the campus network?
- What is the IT policy when law enforcement subpoenas electronic transactions?
- What happens in a computer lab outside the library's purview if a student is viewing what some believe to be pornography?

In fact, all library policies on intellectual freedom need to be discussed with IT departments to ensure there is no policy conflict.

Although in most cases ALA intellectual freedom policy treats Internet content like other formats, legal experts are still debating whether traditional laws of copyright and freedom of expression can be applied to the Internet. The Internet does differ in some important ways. Internet content can be duplicated and transmitted quickly; it is ephemeral in many cases and thus is a challenge to archive; and it can cross national and other civic boundaries, invoking varying regimes of law and creating conflict related to interlibrary loan, hate speech statutes, and data transfer (just to name a few important examples). Copies of content may not be uniform, and not all Internet sites are equally authoritative. Because Internet content is not a fixed medium, its creation, storage, authentication, and distribution differ greatly from that of fixed media. The discourse surrounding this important legal issue is likely to continue for decades.

OVERARCHING PRINCIPLES OF INTELLECTUAL FREEDOM PERTAINING TO THE INTERNET

As it became evident that digital communication was going to revolutionize library collections, access, and services, the U.S. library community advocated the use of the Internet as a powerful tool with the potential to democratize information delivery. At the same time, librarians realized that the very same power would create censorship and privacy challenges. And so the ALA Intellectual Freedom Committee began creating policies and strategies to guide librarians as they, along with the entire country, tried to define and incorporate the Internet into their lives. At just the right time, the Supreme Court emerged in June 1997 with a revolutionary decision in *Reno v. ACLU*.

Reno v. ACLU (521 U.S. 844 [1997])

No decision could have been more crucial and timely to the development of Internet use in libraries. The Supreme Court struck down two provisions of the 1996 Communications Decency Act (CDA) because they violated the freedom of speech clause of the First Amendment in being overly broad. This case was also a landmark because it was the first major Supreme Court ruling about Internet content.

During the Court's deliberations, there was much discussion about whether the Internet was more like the radio and thus should be subject to FCC regulation. The conclusion that the Internet should be afforded the highest First Amendment protection was one of the most crucial judicial decisions of the late twentieth century. The Court reasoned that Internet content is not time sensitive like radio or television—that using the Internet requires more deliberation, interaction, and more steps. Thus, it is more like a book than a radio.

The Court also concluded that the CDA was overly broad because, in its effort to block content inappropriate for children, it blocked content that for adults was protected by the First Amendment. Robert Peck assesses the lasting importance of this decision:

> What *Reno* and its progeny teach are that laws or practices that attempt to limit Internet access out of a concern for juvenile innocence
>
> 1. cannot adversely affect adult access to the same material,
> 2. *must respect the right of access of older minors who are near-adults* [emphasis added; an especially important issue for academic librarians because many college students are minors],
> 3. must respect the rights of parents who choose to permit their children to access sites that others might deem appropriate only for more mature individuals,
> 4. cannot rely on a defense that the access that is denied might be had in other fora, and
> 5. must be evaluated for constitutional purposes in the same highly free-speech protective manner that restrictions on access to newspapers and books are.[2]

Finally, the Court resoundingly envisioned the Internet as a catalyst for democratic discourse: "Through the use of chat rooms, any person with a phone line can become a town crier with a voice that resonates farther than it could from any soapbox. Through the use of web pages, mail exploders, and newsgroups, the same individual can become a pamphleteer."

Reno v. ACLU remains one of the groundbreaking cases for the library profession. For academic librarians it provides support for working with young adults in an open information environment that includes the Internet as a key research tool.

ALA Policies

ACRL Intellectual Freedom Principles for Academic Libraries

6. Open and unfiltered access to the Internet should be conveniently available to the academic community in a college or university library. Content filtering devices and content-based restrictions are a contradiction of the academic library mission to further research and learning through exposure to the broadest possible range of ideas and information. Such restrictions are a fundamental violation of intellectual freedom in academic libraries.

Intellectual Freedom Manual, 7th ed. (Chicago: American Library Association, 2006), 166–68, or www.ala.org/ala/aboutala/offices/oif/statementspols/statementsif/interpretations/intellectual.cfm.

Access to Electronic Information, Services, and Networks: An Interpretation of the Library Bill of Rights

This interpretation is long, complex, and integral to Internet policy formulation in any type of library. The major values promoted are rights of users, equity of access, and the importance of Internet information resources and access to them.

Electronic resources provide unprecedented opportunities to expand the scope of information available to users. Libraries and librarians should provide access to information presenting all points of view. The provision of access does not imply sponsorship or endorsement. These principles pertain to electronic resources no less than they do to the more traditional sources of information in libraries.

Intellectual Freedom Manual, 84–88, or www.ala.org/ala/aboutala/offices/oif/statementsif/ interpretations/intellectual.cfm.

Guidelines and Considerations for Developing a Public Library Internet Use Policy

This document can easily be applied to academic library policy formulation. The first section addresses the public forum doctrine, covered in chapter 4 of this book. The second defines *obscenity, child pornography,* and *harmful to minors.* The third advises librarians about how much authority they should exercise in enforcing obscenity laws. The fourth discusses filters, and the conclusion offers practical guidelines for the kinds of policies and issues public libraries should address. Academic libraries would do well to consult this list and check off each item as it is added to their policy manual.

Intellectual Freedom Manual, 344–51, or www.ala.org/ala/aboutala/offices/oif/statementspols/ otherpolicies/guidelinesconsiderations.cfm.

Privacy Policies

ALA privacy policies are in chapter 5 of this book, and they are also closely related to Internet services, access, and content.

Libraries and the Internet Toolkit

This toolkit is geared more to special issues with younger children, but the guidelines on writing library Internet policy are well worth reviewing.

www.ala.org/ala/aboutala/offices/oif/iftoolkits/toolkitsprivacy.cfm.

OTHER TOOLS AND STRATEGIES FOR ACADEMIC LIBRARIANS

- Local campus IT and library Internet use policies should be reviewed for consistency.
- Campus codes of conduct and faculty handbooks may include Internet use policies.
- Campus intellectual property policies should be reviewed in relationship to Internet use policies, because inevitably there are clashes.
- The library and campus law enforcement should have regular meetings to discuss the library's Internet policies.
- Collect campus Internet use policies from peer institutions. Some public library policies are excellent and can be adapted for academic libraries.
- Collect your state and local laws and statutes regarding the Internet and minors.
- Applicable federal laws should be collected and legislation monitored. See the ALA website for frequent updates.

"A ten-year-old is looking at child pornography over there on that terminal. Call the police."

A summer college prep program assigns its high school student participants to do research in the college library, which has unfiltered Internet access. The reference staff is concerned because the high school students are using their new-found freedom from the filtered public library terminals downtown to access all those sites forbidden to them at the public library. In fact, an older library patron complains to the reference librarian and asks him to call the police.

For academic libraries open to the general community and to minors participating in special programs, unfiltered access to minors may be one of the most difficult intellectual freedom situations we encounter. Librarians are not supposed to be placed in the position of policing what people read or view. In earlier times, what the library purchased was usually legal for the library to possess. Further, even if a library user viewed questionable material at a library table, chances were that the librarian and other users never saw it. Now, with "in your face" screens, Internet content is sometimes impossible to ignore.

For this case I acknowledge the policy at the Fort Vancouver Regional Public Library, Washington, as an invaluable guide, because it covers a very real situation in a very practical way.

Develop Written Procedures and Train the Staff

The library should have procedures in place for the type of event described above, because it is increasingly common. These procedures should have been reviewed with all library staff and with the campus police. In the absence of preparation, a well-meaning staff member might call the city police, for example, when a situation should be handled internally on campus.

The library's posted and written policies should include (1) a statement of the library's mission and (2) a statement that the library's Internet terminals *cannot be used for viewing or downloading obscenity, and that following that rule is the responsibility of the library user.* This policy could even be posted on the Internet terminal if necessary. Remember that "obscenity" can be determined only in a court, so a librarian, police official, or attorney cannot decide. Further, posting that rule protects the library in the case of lawsuit—the library is doing due diligence.

Child pornography is a different story. Child pornography is illegal and relatively easy to identify, and I provide some guidelines below. Librarians are advised to check with their district attorney about state and other statutes relevant to child pornography.

In legal terms, once a user has begun a search session, he or she might be searching the Internet on a system outside the library. Thus the library is not liable for what is being searched. This, of course, depends on how the Internet is set up in your institution, and your IT department can advise you on this.

Know Your Definitions

Three types of materials are often involved in complaints:

> *Obscenity.* This is a legal term, and materials can be determined to be obscene only by a court of law.

Harmful to minors. Currently there is no enforceable federal "harmful to minors" law. You *must* check your state laws to see if there is one in your state. If you have questions, contact your state library.

Child pornography. Many states have child pornography laws and you *must* check your state laws to see if this is the case. There is also a federal law: (18 U.S.C. §2256). There is a definition of *child pornography,* and although it, like *obscenity,* must ultimately be determined by a court of law, there are some images that are easily determined to be child pornography. If a librarian or patron inadvertently sees what he or she believes to fit that definition, then it must be acted upon. At the time of the writing of this book, any depiction of children in sexually explicit conduct is child pornography and is illegal to view. Nudity alone is not child pornography.

It is important that librarians and other frontline personnel know these definitions. It is easy—for both librarians and patrons—to get caught up in an emotional reaction. Some material on the Internet is disturbing and legal for adults to view in libraries. Some is not—for minors or for adults. You must have a clear head to try to work with the patrons and law enforcement if this should become an issue.

If a Library Internet User Is Reported Viewing Child Pornography

Respect the privacy of all involved, and try to speak to the complainant privately. Ask if they can describe the image they saw. The key here is to discern if sexually explicit activity is depicted. Tell the complainant you are going to look into this matter immediately and thank them.

Call the person in charge of the building, which should be listed on the staff procedures.

Remember that in the case of child pornography it is illegal for anyone of any age to view it, whether a ten-year-old or a college senior or a faculty member.

It is OK for a librarian to then approach the patron and see if the image is clearly child pornography. It must be an image of a *real child*. An adult image is not necessarily illegal. A cartoon is not necessarily illegal.

Tell the person that what they are viewing is possibly illegal and that they must close the site immediately. In a recent case at my library, the librarian was able to suggest to a very young patron that she look at some other sites as an alternative, rather than kick her out of the library. The patron is asked to leave only if refusing to cooperate or otherwise acting in a lewd manner.

Remember that downloading or printing child pornography is illegal and you must call the police. Call your IT department to secure the information on the terminal so that the search session will be saved. If the police ask to remove the terminal, tell them that you need a court-ordered subpoena but that you will secure the terminal in the meantime. Put an out-of-order sign on the terminal and turn off the monitor, but not the computer.

In such a situation it is easy to panic. There should always be a "panic button" for someone uneasy with handling the situation. Assure staff that they are not responsible or legally liable for a patron's illegal behavior. Only the patron is responsible. The staff member is not responsible for monitoring patron use of the Internet. But if a staff member sees it accidentally, then it must be reported. ∎

CASE STUDY 2

"Using the Internet terminals to play computer games is inappropriate in academic libraries."

The librarian in charge of the information commons sees a line of students waiting to use the terminals. She sees a student playing computer games and asks her to leave so that another student can use the terminal for her course-related homework.

Academic librarians know that certain times of the year, especially during exams or "reading week," computer workstations are in high demand. Not only is it legally prudent to have a written, standard way to handle high demand—it is easier for all concerned.

To avoid accusations of discrimination, it is far easier to have written policies so that all users and waiters are treated equitably and the librarian can show a user the policy. For example, during times of high demand some libraries give priority to a predefined "primary user community." This might well be the faculty, students, and administration of the school. The key is to predetermine this user group, state the policy in writing, and have a way to identify members of that community.

In this time of curricular innovation, it is unwise for a librarian to try to determine what is "academic" and what is "nonacademic" use of the Internet. There are now undergraduate majors in computer game design and theory, so gaming might be an appropriate use. Also, social networking and software are critical sources of information. It is far better to apportion the computers according to a timesheet and make no judgment about what content the patron is consulting. One also wants to avoid violating patron privacy.

If there is an absolute necessity, libraries can legally set limitations on the type of activity allowed on computer terminals. For example, some libraries prohibit the use of library terminals for e-mail. But remember that any prohibitions must extend to all users. Thus it is still far better to use a neutral control such as time allocation. *The key principle is to respect content neutrality.*

A timesheet can be filled out by those waiting for a terminal. This should be kept behind the desk in the interest of privacy, or a student can use a phony first name to avoid revealing personally identifiable information.

If you are a government document depository library, certain access is required by law (Title 44 of the U.S. Code). Now that many libraries have implemented the CALEA guidelines (see chapter 5), remember that some terminals must be made available to the general public so that they can view government documents. Contact your systems librarian or IT department to make the necessary adjustments and remember that the public must be able to obtain this access at all times the library is open, even when there is no librarian to assist them. ■

"The guy next to me is viewing Nazi stuff on the Web and it offends me."

An international student from Germany complains to the reference librarian that a student at the neighboring workstation is viewing Nazi memorabilia on an auction website. He asks the librarian to call the police.

Nazi memorabilia or current neo-Nazi websites present an important complexity in academic libraries. Even in the most authoritarian regimes around the world, the central national library is often permitted to collect controversial materials. Such materials are often kept in a locked area of the library and are accessible only to scholars with special clearance. During and shortly after World War II, for example, the University of Illinois at Urbana-Champaign was a depository for Nazi government publications. Today this material is rare and unique (much was destroyed during and after the war), so it is kept in a special collection. The Anti-Defamation League has a comprehensive collection of Nazi and neo-Nazi pamphlets in order to educate people about the subject of racial and ethnic hatred and also to document that this material was indeed published. The Jewish Theological Seminary in New York City holds David Irving's controversial book supporting Holocaust denial, presumably because it is a research library and scholars might use it illustratively, not to promote the ideas contained therein.

Germany, France, and other countries have national laws prohibiting Nazi symbols and the sale of Nazi memorabilia on the Internet within their borders. Such laws could cause problems for scholars traveling to professional conferences in these countries. A PowerPoint presentation containing Nazi symbols from books that are perfectly legal in the United States, for example, might cause problems in other countries, and conference participants would do well to check with a campus attorney before sending such materials over the Internet to a country with such laws.

In the United States, Nazi images are permitted in any format and on the Internet. This material is disturbing to many users, and international faculty and students are sometimes unfamiliar with the openness of U.S. library collections policies. If a user complains, a librarian might explain that this material is legal to view in this country and offer the user another workstation location. Another strategy is to install privacy screens on the library's public terminals. You might also explain why the library collects Nazi materials. At the University of Illinois, when I showed the Nazi textbook collection to international library school students, some were upset that a library of UI's stature would house such "trash." It is important to explain that what U.S. libraries collect in no way reflects the personal views of the library or of those who work in it. In some countries where library collections are subject to government control, or where the population has suffered the direct impact of war, this concept may be difficult and painful to accept.

Of course, if a group of students is viewing such materials and intentionally trying to provoke or harass people at neighboring workstations, that must be stopped—regardless of the content. This type of activity is disruption and should be forbidden in written library policies. ■

"We're a private institution and you're not a member of our community; you can't have access to the Internet here."

The president of the local branch of the National Association for the Advancement of Colored People goes to the library lobby help desk and asks for help in finding Internet resources and government documents citing the history of the NAACP. The student staffing the desk asks for a campus ID and then denies the president access to the library.

Private institutions have the right to close their facilities, including libraries, to the general public. Often these libraries have a guard or turnstile to permit only those associated with the campus community. Such regulations are becoming more common as libraries become the sites of increased vandalism and criminal activity.

However, for libraries, public or private, that are designated by Title 44 of the U.S. Code as government document depositories, those collections must be open to the general public. Some libraries have a guard to check people in for specific use of government documents.

Also, most special collections libraries are open to the general public. Often they contain local history collections and are the meeting place for the Library Friends group. Typically these unique collections attract scholars from around the world, and so the library needs to make arrangements for these researchers as well. And many small college libraries serve as their community's resource for the high school Advanced Placement courses.

Wesleyan's Olin Library (and others) have decided that, since there are so many exceptions made for special users and events—and since being open to the general public generates community goodwill—we are open to the general public, with the government document symbol proudly displayed on the front door. We want to encourage local K–12 students to feel comfortable in our building, whether it is for a summer program or a lobby exhibit. This policy is supported by the campus police and the academic administration, who do not want our campus to be viewed by the city residents as a separate "city on the hill."

This open-access policy is not possible for all academic libraries. For those in high-crime areas, it may be necessary to make some arrangements in the interest of public safety. Also, for those colleges located in communities lacking a good public library system, the academic community might need to define its user community more strictly in order to have enough resources to go around. (Ironically, in those cities lacking a good public library, the community is going to need the academic library the most.)

Ideally, libraries should strive to make all materials accessible, regardless of format. Some electronic library collections are password protected because of licensing agreements with periodicals vendors. It is, however, possible to negotiate licenses so that any content on library workstations is available to all, so that there are not first- and second-class users. Unfortunately, this approach may become less available; CALEA (see chapter 5) may require that library computer terminals be password protected, and such authentication requirements would seriously compromise open public access and community relationships. At the time of this writing in late 2008, the terms of CALEA implementation have not been resolved. It is especially important that, if the library is a government depository, print and electronic documents alike must be available to the public along with any finding aids, regardless of format.

It is usually easier for public service librarians on the front line if the library admission policy is as open as possible. Although open public access usually leads to more traffic, exceptions to open access call for extra expense in the form of ID checking or other forms of restriction, including monitoring the reference room. ■

CASE STUDY 5

"In any papers written for my class, you can't cite anything from the Web."

A student tells the reference librarian that she has a research paper assignment and that the professor told the class not to cite the Web in their footnotes.

Some faculty still view the Internet as a collection of junky websites. They need to be informed that the Web is now the source of electronic scholarly journals which, in most cases, have content identical to the print version. Students should be permitted to use and cite such sources in research papers; librarians can provide examples of proper citation. Sometimes information literacy sessions are a great opportunity for librarians to convey this information to faculty and students alike.

Librarians in information literacy or reference transactions do not impose their personal views on students; they can, however, guide students to those library resources considered to be the most appropriate for a particular research need. Often that means that librarians show students which Internet resources are peer reviewed, have been reviewed in professional literature, or have been authenticated by a set of criteria. Librarians know that the Web now contains peer-reviewed journals along with fan clubs and other "fun" sites that might be inappropriate for scholarly projects.

Librarians should use information literacy sessions to explain how to evaluate websites. One of my colleagues likes to say that all information is biased, and that it is the librarian's role to help students figure out how to find the bias. The sponsorship of the website is a good clue; other clues are the advisory board members and the regular contributors. ∎

NOTES

1. *Internet Filters: A Public Policy Report,* 2nd ed. (New York: Brennan Center for Justice at NYU School of Law, 2006), ii. The report can be downloaded from www.brennancenter.org.
2. Robert S. Peck, *The First Amendment and Cyberspace* (Chicago: American Library Association, 2000), 132.

CHAPTER 4

Library Exhibit Spaces, Programs, and Rooms

The Academic Library as Agora

The agora, typified by the heart of ancient Athens, was simultaneously the locus of commercial, political, administrative, social, religious, and cultural activity, and citizens freely participated in the range of activities. . . . [Philosophers later applied the concept to] dissemination on and discussion of ideas, arguing that broad social benefits are produced when information and expression of the independent ideas of citizens are permitted.

R. Schmuhl and R. G. Picard, "The Marketplace of Ideas"

One of the major conversations about academic libraries these days is how to define them. Are they "book boxes"? Are they places for undergraduates to pick up Friday night dates? Are they glorified computer labs or big study halls? Several recent conferences and publications have struggled with these questions. The University of Rochester Library has its own staff ethnographer, whom many libraries have hired to conduct ethnographic research on exactly how their faculty, students, and staff utilize library space. And the answers may surprise you.

As described in this book's introduction, today's academic libraries are social spaces as well as individual research spaces. "Millennial" students still insist on having private, cozy places to curl up with a book made of paper. At the same time, many use group study rooms for collaborative projects. Wesleyan University's Olin Library ground floor is affectionately called "Club Olin" by the students, and the librarians will never know exactly why. That is the point. We do know that they sit on the floor together, even if chairs are available.

At Wesleyan, as on many campuses, Olin Library is prime real estate. The stunning lobby, designed by Lincoln Memorial architect Henry Bacon, is used for a variety of performance and exhibit art. One week Tibetan monks created a sand mandala in the lobby, amid wide Middletown community participation to celebrate its completion. Another week the lobby had an art installation of two wooden closets—one marked "blacks only" and the other "whites only." Students could sit in the booths and record their feelings about race. After the Indian Ocean tsunami of 2004, Olin Library worked with student organizations to display all affected countries' flags, accompanied by a multimedia tape with photos and music from Wesleyan's world music archives.

The gay, lesbian, and transgender community wrapped the library's exterior columns in rainbow cloth to celebrate Gay Pride. An art professor and students created a provocative exhibit that involved sticking call numbers all over the library and community buildings. For example, the exit security gate bore the call number for Sartre's play *No Exit*. Recently, the Library Friends hosted Amos Paul Kennedy Jr., a handpress poster artist whose work is now exhibited for sale in the lobby: "A Dirty Book Is Seldom Dusty."

And yes, the Library hosts very traditional lectures to honor Constitution Day.

For Wesleyan University, it is fitting that the library be an integral part of the world-famous arts curriculum. It builds good library visibility with the rest of campus, and it furthers the campus mission to foster good community relationships and global awareness. Wesleyan's library, though private, has decided to be an *agora*—the Greek word for a marketplace. The library is a marketplace of ideas. Though private, it functions like a designated public forum, where visitors have the right to receive ideas. And they are given all sorts of ways to receive them.

None of the above activities ruffled any campus feathers. But some of the banners hung from the balconies during one trustees meeting did. And so did a Japanese drumming concert that disturbed quiet study in the Campbell Reading Room. Wesleyan student demonstrators, rambunctious high school students, and outbursts of mentally disturbed visitors have also caused anxiety. One exhibit, intentionally scattered around the lobby, prompted more than one library user to assume it was litter and throw it away.

Some campus colleagues believe that libraries should retain the grandeur of Henry Bacon's day, when libraries were truly palaces of learning. These are the kinds of arguments, risks, and problems that accompany a space used as a limited public forum. It is much easier to limit library use, especially when there is a good excuse—after all, the university is a private institution.

But the Wesleyan campus community has decided that it is worth the risk in order to enliven the library. Donors are seldom attracted to empty buildings, and Olin Library is empty only some mornings—but packed at 10:00 p.m. There is a lot of talk on other campuses these days about whether academic libraries are outmoded, underutilized, and worth any further investment, and librarians must take such discussions very seriously.

How does a lively library space work successfully? First, one must have community consensus on how the space will be used. Second, there must be written policies for the use of all library spaces, from various rooms, to the lobby, to bulletin boards, to exhibit cases. Third, librarians must be prepared for controversy and ready to turn it into opportunities for community discussions about freedom of expression. These discussions might be with students, but they could also be with the campus police.

Because academic libraries have the potential of being agoras, it is important for librarians to understand the concept of "public forum." This is particularly true for librarians in publicly funded colleges or universities, but even librarians in private institutions will find the definitions helpful as they develop library space use policies. Also, ALA's Code of Ethics applies to librarians in all types of institutions and underlies all ALA space use policies.

THE PUBLIC FORUM DOCTRINE

One expert and accessible analysis of the public forum doctrine applied to libraries is by Theresa Chmara, partner at Jenner and Block, a law firm based in Washington, D.C.[1] Chmara is also counsel for ALA's Freedom to Read Foundation. Chmara emphasizes the corollary to the First Amendment right to speak—the right to receive information. This right to receive information means that librarians do not exist simply to protect the collections from censorship. The library information literacy program, interlibrary loan, and other services that enhance user access are thus activities that promote First Amendment principles and academic freedom and are an integral part of a lively public forum.

There are three different types of public forums and First Amendment tests for each. For example, the *traditional public forum* of a soapbox in a public park has always been protected by the First Amendment under *strict scrutiny* standards. In other words, if the government tries to restrict speech in such a place, the government must prove that the restrictions serve a *compelling state interest* and are narrowly defined. Otherwise, speech that should be protected by the First Amendment might be inadvertently hindered.

On the other end of the spectrum is the *nonpublic forum.* One good example is the White House, much of which is always closed to the public. A library could define itself as a nonpublic forum. This means that no outside groups could meet there, except perhaps the Library Friends; any and all requests of such groups as the Young Democrats or the Young Republicans would be refused. Nonpublic forums are allowed to be more selective and restrictive in regard to content, but if that status is ever challenged by a library user courts look for written policies to support the nonpublic forum status.

A *designated* or *limited public forum* sits in the middle of this spectrum. Recent court cases have placed publicly funded libraries in this category. What does this mean for publicly funded academic libraries?

The government (in many cases, the state government) has designated the campus library not only for containing books but also for allowing speech and the receipt of information by its users. Nonetheless, certain restrictions can still be established for use of this type of library space.

The library, once it has been defined as a designated public forum, must be careful about content-based restrictions, because those restrictions are subject to First

Amendment scrutiny. The library must be certain that *time, place,* and *manner restrictions* (see below) are narrowly tailored and content neutral. For example, the library can prohibit all barefoot patrons because of insurance restrictions; that prohibition has nothing to do with content. Or the library can establish hours of operation, before or after which the library cannot be used by anyone. If some faculty or students are granted special after-hours keys, that is arguably a violation.

As Chmara states, when crafting policies, "library officials must ensure that the policies are (1) written, (2) objective, (3) consistently enforced, (4) reasonable and related to library use, and (5) accompanied by an appeal mechanism, even if that mechanism is informal."[2] When library public access is limited in any way, the key is that in the application of the library's written policies there is no perceived or actual discrimination on the basis of content. Also, patrons must be treated equitably in terms of federal and other civil rights laws.

TIME, PLACE, AND MANNER RESTRICTIONS

The courts have discussed *time, place,* and *manner restrictions* in several important cases. Even librarians in private institutions will find this analysis helpful for guidance and assurance of providing equitable access to their user community. Time, place, and manner restrictions can be imposed on speech that is ordinarily protected by the First Amendment, as long as the restrictions are content neutral and applied as such. For libraries, time, place, and manner restrictions mean that a library can be a designated public forum and still have some rules and policies, as long as they are content neutral. Time restrictions include the right of a library to have hours and not be open all night—as long as these hours apply to all users. Place restrictions mean, for example, that a library can establish quiet zones where verbally expressed speech is not allowed—by anyone. Manner restrictions mean, for example, that the library can prohibit loud music played on its computer workstations; such a restriction must, however, be content neutral. Classical and hip-hop music are both subject to the same policy.

The key questions to ask when preparing library programming include the above considerations plus the following:

- Is your institution private or public?
- How has the library been used in the past? Are there written policies about use by outside groups and for nonlibrary purposes? Do you have an application form to be filled out by all who wish to use your library space?
- Have the written polices been vetted recently for potential civil rights violations or inequities regarding content or point of view? Have you received any complaints, and how have you responded?

For librarians just beginning to develop library programming, some broad questions should be pondered. What is the purpose of the programs? For example, many academic libraries are working closely with their campus administration to enhance town/gown relationships. Perhaps the college is keen on having an impact on K–12 education in the region. Campuswide impact should be integral to library decisions about how "public" to make the library space.

Many academic libraries have developed policies that define a primary user group to be served first. For example, many libraries do not answer community reference questions until students, faculty, and staff needs are satisfied. Such policies are allowed

Public Forum Doctrine and the Library

A *public forum* is a public space or government-owned property in which the public can exercise the First Amendment right to speak or receive ideas. *Public forum doctrine* is the set of rules developed by the courts to identify a public forum and to define the scope of First Amendment protections extended to those using a public forum for expressive activities.

The Supreme Court has identified two kinds of public forums. The first is the *traditional public forum,* a place "held in trust for the use of the public and, time out of mind, . . . used for purposes of assembly, communicating thoughts between citizens, and discussing public questions," such as parks, sidewalks, and public squares. The second is the *designated public forum,* property that the government has intentionally opened for expressive activity by part or all of the public (*Perry Educ. Ass'n v. Perry Local Educators' Ass'n*).

A designated public forum can be opened to all expressive activity, like a traditional public forum, or opened only on a limited basis to particular groups, or for particular speech activities. In deciding whether a government agency has created a designated public forum, courts examine the policies and practices of the agency to determine if the agency intended to open a place not traditionally open for free speech activities for use as a public forum.

In a public forum, the government may not restrict speech based solely on its content unless it can show that the restriction is necessary to achieve a compelling government interest; that the restriction is narrowly drawn to achieve that interest; and that there are no less restrictive alternatives available that can accomplish the government's goal.

The government can, however, make content-neutral rules that regulate the time, place, and manner of speech in a public forum. Such rules must be narrowly drawn to serve an important government interest and must operate without regard for the identity of the individual, the content of the individual's speech, or the viewpoint expressed by the individual.

In its opinion in *Kreimer v. Bureau of Police,* the Third Circuit Court of Appeals ruled unequivocally that the public library is a designated public forum. Applying public forum doctrine to determine the limitations on the library's ability to limit access to the library, the court held that the Morristown Public Library created a designated public forum when it intentionally opened the library to the public for the specified purposes of reading, studying, and using the library's materials. Because the library had not opened its doors for other speech activities, such as speechmaking or passing out pamphlets, the court found that the library was a limited public forum, open only for those expressive activities consistent with the nature of the library and the right to access information.

In accord with public forum doctrine, the *Kreimer* court ruled the library, as a limited public forum, was required to permit only expressive activities that facilitate the receipt of information and could establish reasonable rules designed to promote safety or efficient access to the library's materials to regulate nonexpressive activity. Thus, the library could have a rule allowing librarians to remove persons with extremely offensive bodily hygiene that unreasonably interferes with other persons' use of the library.

The analysis used by the *Kreimer* court continues to be used by courts to decide cases concerning access to libraries and library materials. For example, in the case of *Sund v. City of Wichita Falls,* the court struck down an ordinance allowing library card holders to require the library to remove a book from the children's section and place it in the adult section, on the grounds that the library, as a limited public forum, could not "limit access to library materials solely on the basis of the content of those materials, unless the City can demonstrate that the restriction is necessary to achieve a compelling government interest and there are no less restrictive alternatives for achieving that interest."

In *Neinast v. Bd. of Trustees of the Columbus Metro. Library,* the Sixth Circuit Court of Appeals relied on public forum doctrine to uphold a library regulation that required library users to wear shoes in the library. The court held that, although the library was a limited public forum for the receipt of information, it could reasonably require that its users wear shoes as a health and safety matter, since the rule was a narrowly drawn, content-neutral regulation that was reasonable in light of reports demonstrating that hazardous materials had been found on the library's floor.

But in *Armstrong v. D.C. Public Library,* the court struck down a library regulation that allowed librarians to remove anyone whose appearance a librarian regarded as "objectionable." The court found that there was no standard to determine what was "objectionable" and held that, as a result, the rule "threatens to compromise access to information and ideas found within the Library's limited public forum by directly precluding, or otherwise discouraging, use of the D.C. Public Library system by persons that Library staff, in their discretion, find objectionable."

These cases and other library precedents developed under the public forum doctrine are invaluable guidance for publicly funded college and university libraries that desire to develop access and use policies consistent with the First Amendment, as well as private university libraries that wish to adopt and emulate First Amendment principles.

Additional Resources

Armstrong v. D.C. Public Library, 154 F. Supp. 2d 67 (D.D.C. 2001)

Kreimer v. Bureau of Police, 958 F.2d 1242 (3d Cir. 1992)

Neinast v. Bd. of Trustees of the Columbus Metro. Library, 346 F.3d 585 (6th Cir. 2003)

Perry Educ. Ass'n v. Perry Local Educators' Ass'n, 460 U.S. 37 (1983)

Sund v. City of Wichita Falls, 121 F. Supp. 2d 530 (N.D. Tex. 2000)

There are universities that don't allow certain kinds of speakers on campus. There are universities that put restriction on the ability of student organizations to invite people to campus. And so on the scale of free speech at universities, we are way over to the most permissive, the most open side. We don't have a speech code; we don't want one. We aren't afraid of controversy; we in fact welcome controversy. We aren't afraid of speakers that might offend students, because we think from most speakers there is something to be learned. So that's our policy, and that's our tradition. And it makes for a turbulent community sometimes. That's both the price and the benefit of our values and our policies.

*University provost Alan Brinkley,
Columbia University*[3]

in a designated, limited public forum, as long as these restrictions are written and applied equitably; librarians might want to think twice, however, before enforcing such a rule if it has a negative impact on community relations.

One common campus problem arises over controversial speakers (as noted in the Columbia University/Ahmadinejad affair, chapter 1). If the library has invited such a speaker, campus security should be alerted to the potential for campus unrest. The library should do whatever it can to convince the campus that it is worth the additional overtime or security forces to save the program from cancellation. The public relations repercussions can be severe when free speech is chilled for whatever reason, and the local press may suppose that the campus does not really support academic freedom.

CAMPUS FREE-SPEECH ZONES

Some public universities have established campus free-speech zones. Some campuses have placed these in libraries. The First Amendment Center's research attorney, David L. Hudson Jr., has prepared a thorough analysis of such zones.[4] He points out that some public universities established such zones as a way to limit student protest and demonstration to particular areas of campus. Such zones are also a response to the fact that the courts have been striking down speech codes (see the introduction to this book).

Some campus administrators argue that free-speech zones are a way to prevent activism from interfering with the pedagogical function of universities. Some campuses have moved demonstrations to particular zones for the purpose of safety and to prevent congestion. Further, they argue, such zones are content neutral and therefore can hold up to the most stringent judicial review, including time, place, and manner restrictions.

A public forum analysis of free-speech zones at public institutions might go somewhat like this. Some argue that the public forum doctrine is ill defined. One could argue that the main purpose of academic institutions is classroom teaching, and speech not related to that mission should be limited to particular zones. These zones, like a library, simply regulate where the speech takes place. They do not prohibit the speech from taking place at all. Other college presidents worry that the existence of free-speech zones implies that other parts of campus are not free-speech zones. This could cause problems for performances, classroom discussions, and library programs, services, and content.

One interesting case arose at West Virginia University, where the university established seven free-speech zones. In the 2002 case *Free Speech Coalition of West Virginia University v. Hardesty*, students alleged that their First Amendment rights were violated because they could exercise free speech in only 5 percent of the campus area. They further alleged that the zones were placed intentionally in areas in which the protest would have minimal impact. For example, demonstrations were prohibited at the Center for Black Culture and Research and in front of the student newspaper building. In December 2002, the university abandoned its policy.

The Foundation for Individual Rights in Education, a Philadelphia civil liberties organization, opposes such zones. Many academics, including Robert O'Neil of the Thomas Jefferson Center for the Protection of Free Expression, located at the University of Virginia, agree. They believe that such zones restrict speech to certain places and thus hinder the "marketplace of ideas" approach. O'Neil, a well-known expert on campus free-speech issues, states that free-speech zones, "while seeming to be content-neutral, can create a content effect. While seemingly content-neutral, when you look deeper some of the policies seem to mask content discrimination."[5]

Some attorneys argue that there may be ways to craft a free-speech zone policy that passes muster in regard to the public forum doctrine. It is important for librarians to know where their college or university stands, so that the administration understands that library space supportive of academic freedom and the First Amendment is core to its primary mission.

OVERARCHING PRINCIPLES OF INTELLECTUAL FREEDOM PERTAINING TO LIBRARY SPACE FOR PROGRAMMING

Exhibit Spaces and Bulletin Boards: An Interpretation of the Library Bill of Rights

Exhibits should be developed like any other type of library collection or service. Written policies are essential in order to define the groups allowed to use the space. Also, time, place, and manner restrictions can be applied. The space can be limited to use by the members of the academic community, but within that community no exhibit should be turned down because of content (unless it contains speech unprotected by the First Amendment). Just as the library does not necessarily support all points of view in the collections, the same is true for topics in exhibits. The library can restrict exhibits to particular spaces, and it can establish time limits in order to allow as many groups as possible to exhibit in the space.

Intellectual Freedom Manual, 7th ed. (Chicago: American Library Association, 2006), 140–41, or www.ala.org/ala/aboutala/offices/oif/statementspols/statementspolicies.cfm.

Library-Initiated Programs as a Resource: An Interpretation of the Library Bill of Rights

The same time, place, and manner restrictions apply to library programming as to exhibits, bulletin boards, and meeting rooms. The library should strive for a diversity of programming. Most important, library programming is a wonderful way to engage the greater community and to get them to visit campus.

Intellectual Freedom Manual, 182–86, or www.ala.org/ala/aboutala/offices/oif/statementspols/statementspolicies.cfm.

Meeting Rooms: An Interpretation of the Library Bill of Rights

Meeting rooms should be subject to written applications and policies, as are exhibition spaces and bulletin boards. They are subject to time, place, and manner restrictions, and the content of the meetings or the beliefs of the participants should not be an issue. If the library opens its rooms to the general community and includes civic organizations, then it cannot exclude religious or political organizations; libraries are advised to investigate the current status of court rulings regarding the distinction between religious-themed meetings and religious services held in library meeting space. Publicly funded institutions can restrict their library meeting rooms to library-related activities. The library policy should be consistent in regard to whether the meetings can be open to all or closed to members only.

Intellectual Freedom Manual, 187–88, or www.ala.org/ala/aboutala/offices/oif/statementspols/statementspolicies.cfm.

CHECKLIST OF TOOLS OR ISSUES TO ADDRESS

When you are developing policies and procedures for the use of library space for exhibitions, meetings, and programs, this checklist of issues may be helpful:

- Is the library public or private?
- Does the campus have a free-speech code?
- Does the campus have free-speech zones?
- Is there any reference to use of the library in the student code of conduct or similar campus policy?
- Do the library and the campus security department hold regular meetings about upcoming library activities?
- Has your campus adopted an academic freedom statement?
- Are there written library policies for meeting rooms, exhibits, and programs, based on the above criteria in the *Intellectual Freedom Manual*?
- Is there a written application process for use of library space, with copies of library policies attached?

CONCLUSION

Many library directors decide to place the library off limits for many types of activities, because it is too hard to make some of the complex decisions that go along with programming in a designated public forum. Further, there is always the risk that opening up the library might inadvertently create discrimination or other unforeseen problems. This is particularly frustrating if the campus administration is unwilling to support the library's programming philosophy. Nonetheless, some librarians find that a more open library space is worth the risk. This use of the library can create enormous goodwill with faculty, students, alumni, and administration—not to mention the larger community. Because many campus libraries are underutilized and because campus resources are limited, it may be worth the effort to create library programs that ensure a busy, energized space.

For many libraries the occasional unruly patron has been a minor problem in exchange for such popular programs as Wesleyan's recent Tibetan monks creating the sand mandala for the entire community. To use an academic library as a public forum is to make the library the intellectual heart of the campus—not only for the books it contains but also for the exchange of ideas. This is an opportunity for librarians to market what a library means in the twenty-first century. It is innovative and at the same time mirrors the agora of Greece in the fifth century B.C.

CASE STUDY 1

"This one-week project in the library lobby is religious. What about separation of church and state?"

Note: Although this incident recounts a residency of Buddhist monks whose project was housed in the Wesleyan University library, none of these events occurred. Our program planners anticipated any and all possible problems, and incidents like the fictional one described here could happen, particularly in a publicly funded library.

At a large, private academic university, a group of exiled Tibetan monks take up a one-week residence in the university library. They are using the library lobby to sell monastery crafts for fund-raising. They are also distributing leaflets about the current situation in Tibet, where they are prohibited from practicing their religion. The leaflets clearly criticize the policies of the current Chinese regime in Beijing. The entire town and campus community is involved in various library activities in the library during that week.

The Chinese Student Association complains to the university librarian that the Chinese government's grievances against Tibet have not been expressed and that the monks are presenting only one side of the story. The Secular Humanist Club complains that the exhibit violates the separation of church and state.

Before the monks are invited to campus and before the library agrees to participate, the librarian should be familiar with the public forum doctrine and how it applies to that library. He should obtain campus consensus on the mission and content of the program. He should anticipate potential political issues. In this case study, the private or public status of the institution may make a big difference. Tibetan monks have created sand mandalas in both private and public universities, but it would be useful for the librarian to check for any unanticipated difficulties. For example, one might imagine that, if the monks perform any religious ceremonies at a public university, some might protest that the separation of church and state has been violated. In an institution of higher education, however—even a public institution—the library could probably argue that the ceremony is a demonstration for the purposes of education.

At Wesleyan, a private university, not only could the monks perform a Buddhist ceremony, the library also permits the lighting of Chanukah candles and Christmas caroling—as long as the entire campus community is welcome to all of these ceremonies held in the Olin Library lobby. Public institutions probably have very different policies. The important point is that written policies regarding the use of library space are essential. To be effective, these written policies should obtain campus approval and should be based on the institutional mission and ALA policies and principles.

Librarians should not forget to vet policies about use of library space with campus security officials, so that if crowd control becomes an issue they have been alerted ahead of time.

Unless the library is facing an immediate crisis, the impending arrival of a program is a great time to review library space use policies. ALA's written policies in this area provide a great deal of guidance. Space use policies should include paper or online forms for requesting permission to use library space. There should also be a transparent process for making decisions about use of library space. The library director, or delegate, should review library programming annually to make sure that there has been a relatively balanced and diverse representation of campus groups and interests.

Some controversies should be anticipated, and even welcomed—though a library director always feels better amid controversy if he or she is prepared. It is all too easy to wish for "comfortable" programming in the library. For programs we anticipate will evoke controversy, we should have a procedure in place for communicating with offended students (and even their parents), not to mention alumni and board members who threaten to cut their annual giving. Consider, though, that the opportunities afforded by edgy, tasteful exhibits or performances are exciting, especially now when the United States is so deeply divided on a great number of important issues. Libraries can offer the community a place and means to express their opinions. There is nothing worse than viewing a performance or exhibit, experiencing a powerful emotional response, and then having no way to discuss it. Academe reflects our deeply divided global society and encourages student and faculty discourse. If the Palestinian Student

Organization wants to create an exhibit documenting life in the Occupied Territories, most librarians would anticipate that other campus groups will want an opportunity to respond in kind—and would offer that opportunity.

If an exhibit is predictably inflammatory, there are ways to present it, encourage freedom of expression, and encourage discourse without violence. One way is to ensure a "space" in the program for response. Library speaker programs should include a question-and-answer session and even an informal reception. A blank-paged notebook or blog at an exhibition is another excellent way to give visitors an opportunity to express their views. I recently attended an Amsterdam, Holland, exhibit on Muslim headscarves, and the comments book included deep opposition from secular Muslims, who fear that headscarves foster intolerance from the greater Dutch community. The comments in that book were, indeed, as rich as the exhibit. In the museum gift shop, traditional headscarves were sold as well. Library physical and electronic bulletin boards should provide a space for opposing groups to advertise meetings to present their points of view.

Librarians should decide ahead of time if they are going to allow the sale of merchandise to support any given exhibit. Many libraries sell Friends items. Find out if campus policy allows the selling of crafts and other materials within the library.

Even if all of the above policies and procedures are in order, the library could still miscalculate strong dissatisfaction from one or more groups or individuals. The librarian should talk with the group's representatives and work with them to arrive at a remedy. One suggestion could be a response on the library blog, bulletin board, or newsletter. Another might be an exhibit or performance highlighting the complaining group's perspective. Any complaint should be the impetus for updating current policies (or for writing policies in the first place!). And, while listening to complaints about a particular program, the librarian has a great opportunity to ask if library service and collections in general meet the complainants' needs and represent their point of view. ■

CASE STUDY 2

"Making this movie is a part of my class project, and I need to use the reference room because it is a perfect backdrop."

Six students arrive in the reference room during reading period (near the end of term) and begin to shoot a musical for their final project in a film course. Several students already studying in the reference room complain that they need a quiet place to study and that the filmmakers are disruptive. Who must be forced to move?

Libraries are increasingly used as the backdrop for student senior thesis projects or other assignments—to make a film, to photograph a scene, or even to sing or drum. I was once asked by a student if the film he was making in the library could include the use of fake weapons and fake blood. Olin Library was used for a PBS film recently, but only after the university librarian consulted with campus public relations and made certain that library study and research functions would not be unduly affected. Bobst Library at New York University regularly receives such requests because of its prime location in Greenwich Village and its visual impact. Libraries should have a policy for their use as a general setting for films and performances. Time, place, and manner restrictions make it possible to restrict such uses to particular times of the academic year, when students are not using the library to study for exams or to complete term papers. The library should also have a written policy requiring proper notice before shooting a film. There are several privacy laws and releases that must be signed, and so the library would be within its rights to refuse to give permission to the filmmakers.

If tense relations with the campus film studies department might ensue, if the library does not have written policies and is able to find alternative spaces for the students to conduct their quiet study, then it might want to grant permission to the film students but notify the film studies department that, as of the next academic year, film making will not be allowed without prior permission. Wesleyan has an active film program, and I have found the faculty and administration to be extremely supportive of the library in such situations. The faculty want the students to learn early in their film careers about getting prior permission to use a site, and to understand about privacy waivers as well. The same is true of music students who want to drum in a stairwell to get an echoing effect. The campus wants these students to learn more than just performance skills; they must also learn that they are part of a learning community and need to respect others in that community.

Demonstrations

Demonstrations within a library can be problematic if they disrupt study. Remember that libraries have the right to create policies with time, place, and manner restrictions. One alternative on many campuses is to provide the front steps of the library as a place for candlelight vigils and other means of protest. Most libraries should consider carefully the types of demonstrations it allows within its walls. On a commuter campus, for example, the library may be the only place with quiet places for study. If the library becomes too noisy and disruptive, then it is not fulfilling one of its primary missions. If a demonstration begins spontaneously, campus safety officials should be alerted for crowd control and to control candles or weapons.

Banners

The library has a right to apply time, place, and manner restrictions to limit exhibition of banners. Such restrictions should be content neutral—that is, the prohibition of a banner in a particular place should have nothing to do with the words on that banner. As with any use of library space, there should be an application and approval process. Frequently the visits of dignitaries, including the board of trustees, are a catalyst for protest, posters, and banners. It is important that the library create some sort of space, like a bulletin board or a blog, for the campus community to use as an outlet for expression of concerns. If it does not, vandalism such as graffiti is inevitable.

Pamphleteering

In recent years many libraries have found pamphlets inserted into entire ranges of books. Sometimes these political or religious pamphlets are placed strategically into related subject areas. For example, at Middlebury College anti-Semitic or proselytizing pamphlets were stuck into books in the Israel and Jewish history sections of the stacks. Librarian Barbara Doyle-Wilch was sorry the incident happened but gratified at the campus reaction. Instead of simply enforcing library rules, Doyle-Wilch used this incident as a teachable moment. Two campus groups—Hillel and the Inter-Varsity Christian Fellowship—sat on the floors of the stacks and removed the pamphlets from all the books. Then they had dinner together. Both groups felt it had brought them closer together. One of the campus chaplains reacted:

> It was a rewarding experience for me to see the students of IVCF and Hillel join forces in addressing an affront to Middlebury College's sense of respect for differences among students and religious/ethnic groups on campus. These students took a problematic occurrence and made it into a learning experience of the first order, sharing scholarship and fellowship, while building bridges of mutual understanding and friendship.[6]

Some librarians have asked whether we should, indeed, remove pamphlets. After all, is this not a limitation on freedom of speech? The answer is that, in a limited public forum, the library can establish time, place, and manner restrictions. The collection development policy determines what materials the library has selected. The pamphlets stuck in the books are not part of that policy. So, although it is not mandatory for libraries to remove these pamphlets, it is certainly within their rights to do so.

Librarians in public universities should check the status of such cases as one at New Mexico State University, which adopted a policy in the 1980s that included limitations on pamphleteering to three areas. A case was filed but never went to court: *Rudolph v. Archuleta.* In 2001 the campus modified its policy to say that pamphlets can be distributed in "any outdoor area . . . as long as the primary action is not to advertise or sell a commercial product." ∎

NOTES

1. Theresa Chmara, "Public Libraries and the Public Forum Doctrine," *Intellectual Freedom Manual,* 7th ed. (Chicago: American Library Association, 2006), 369–83.

2. Ibid., 374.

3. Alan Brinkley, quoted in Paul Hond, "Fighting Words," *Columbia,* Winter 2006/7, 14.

4. David L. Hudson Jr., "Free-Speech Zones: Overview," www.firstamendmentcenter.org/speech/pubcollege/. Citations through April 2003.

5. O'Neil quoted in Kevin O'Shea, "Muzzling Campus Speech," in *First Amendment Rights in Education,* May 2002.

6. Zach Hecht-Leavitt, "Hillel, CF Fight Anti-Semitism," *Middlebury Campus: Middlebury College Weekly* (online news), posted November 3, 2005. This weekly can be found at www.middleburycollege.edu or by contacting the College Archives.

CHAPTER 5

Privacy and Confidentiality

Welcome to the monkey house. We're the monkeys and the tourists both—the exhibitionist and the voyeur. Each bar in our cage is smelted from the same metal—technology. If you want privacy, pay cash, send postal mail, use a television antenna, and don't travel by airplane or leave the country. That strategy might work right up until the inevitable national ID card is mandated. Of course, you'll give up many of the benefits of our society; renting cars requires a credit card, for example.

Technology is wonderful. It extends our life span, feeds the poor, and helps us thrive in harsh environments like tundra and deserts. Just as the railroads opened up the United States in the nineteenth century, networked smart devices are opening up new business areas in the twenty-first. But there are consequences. Building the railroads killed off the buffalo. What will building the Information Superhighway kill off?

David Holtzman, *Privacy Lost: How Technology Is Endangering Your Privacy*

Scientific American's September 2008 "The Future of Privacy" theme issue reflects the growing public concern over the security of personally identifiable information.[1] The Federal Trade Commission estimates that over nine million Americans are victims of identity theft annually.[2] Such breaches, along with unauthorized disclosure of medical information, have focused public attention on issues that have concerned librarians and the higher-education sector for decades.

But at the same time that identity theft was reaching alarming proportions, the September 11 attacks brought a stark reminder that terrorists could exploit Internet privacy protections so that their activities could not be traced. The result—a plethora of federal, state, and local antiterrorist legislation that compromises individual privacy in the interest of national security. These laws extend the capabilities of telecommunications companies to wiretap individual transactions on telephones and computers. They also authorize searches of confidential library records without a court-ordered subpoena. Such invasions of personal privacy have a chilling effect on library service.

At the same time, Web 2.0 has introduced social networking capabilities that have been embraced by young adults—and also by libraries as a way to engage a new generation of library users. Studies show that the popularity of such communications tools as blogs, wikis, and Facebook far outweighs any user concern over the very real threat of compromising individual privacy. Even as the ALA begins its three-year privacy awareness initiative with the Open Society Institute, it still encourages librarians to use Facebook, blogs, and other Web 2.0 tools. The ALA project advisory board will appropriately include representatives from not only the Thomas Jefferson Center at the University of Virginia but also Google, Inc.[3]

WHAT IS PRIVACY? CONFIDENTIALITY? ANONYMITY?

For the purposes of this book's focus on higher education, *privacy* is defined as a right—"a right to engage in open inquiry without having the subject of one's interest examined or scrutinized by others." *Confidentiality* is a situation—in which a library or campus library or office "is in possession of personally identifiable information about library users [or other campus constituents] and keeps that information private on their behalf."[4] *Anonymity* is the ideal status of an individual library user in regard to library transactions. It is achieved by the separation of personally identifiable information from the individual's transactions with the library. There is a period of time when anonymity is breached—when a book is checked out, for example. During that period the confidentiality of library records is especially important and the library has a special duty to secure those records in the name of privacy protection. M. Ethan Katsch's summary of the meaning of privacy is particularly applicable to the mission of U.S. higher education: Privacy is

> a condition that allows the individual freedom to choose when to establish a relationship and when not. . . . Privacy needs to be understood as being an inherently pro-choice doctrine in that its goal is to provide the individual with an environment in which he or she can make independent choices.[5]

HOW IS PRIVACY RELATED TO THE FIRST AMENDMENT?

In U.S. legal history, privacy was famously discussed by Louis Brandeis and his law partner, Samuel Warren, in an 1890 *Harvard Law Review* article.[6] Early remedies were sought through tort law. Constitutional law, on the other hand, protects privacy by combining several principles, doctrines, and decisions—even though the word *privacy* does not appear in the U.S. Constitution (it does in several state constitutions). The First Amendment clause protecting *freedom of association* has been used to uphold the privacy of those who do not want to disclose their membership in particular organizations. The Fourth Amendment protects citizens from "searches and seizures," and

Library Records, Privacy, and the First Amendment

The right to privacy in what one reads or views in the library, and the associated right to have the records of those activities kept confidential, is founded on the First Amendment and its protection of the right to read and receive information anonymously.

The principle that anonymity is necessary for the free exercise of First Amendment rights can be traced to the Supreme Court's recognition that the Bill of Rights protects not only the enumerated rights but also the conditions that ensure the uninhibited exercise of those rights. Protecting the right to speak anonymously or read anonymously helps to ensure that no one is discouraged from considering or receiving controversial ideas. As the Supreme Court explained in *McIntyre v. Ohio Elections Commission,* "anonymity is a shield from the tyranny of the majority. It thus exemplifies the purpose behind the Bill of Rights and of the First Amendment in particular: to protect unpopular individuals from retaliation—and their ideas from suppression—at the hand of an intolerant society."

The Supreme Court first protected the right to read anonymously in *Lamont v. Postmaster General,* a decision that struck down as unconstitutional a law requiring individuals to identify themselves in order to receive publications that were allegedly Communist propaganda. The Court's opinion relied on the law's "chilling effect"—its potential to deter individuals from exercising their right to obtain and read controversial materials—as the grounds for overturning the law as an abridgment of First Amendment rights.

A later Supreme Court decision, *Stanley v. Georgia,* famously defended "the right to be free from state inquiry into the contents of [one's] library," when it overturned the conviction of an individual convicted of possessing materials deemed obscene by the State of Georgia. The Court rejected the state's argument that mere possession of disfavored materials justified invading the individual's privacy, asserting that "the right to be free from unwanted governmental intrusions into one's privacy is fundamental."

The result of these and similar court decisions is the recognition that the First Amendment protects the right to read and receive ideas anonymously, free from any government inquiry or interference that might chill the exercise of that right.

In particular, demands by law enforcement or the government to examine records held by a bookstore or library in order to determine what books a person has read (or what websites the person has visited) are viewed by courts as government action that can encroach upon the individual's First Amendment rights.

For example, when independent counsel Ken Starr issued a subpoena to two bookstores to discover the book-buying habits of Monica Lewinsky, the court found that the bookstores had proven that First Amendment interests could be harmed if the subpoena was enforced. The court ruled that, in light of the First Amendment claims made by the bookstores, the government would need to demonstrate a compelling need for the information sought and show a sufficient connection between the information sought and the grand jury investigation before the court would enforce the subpoena (*In re Grand Jury Subpoena to Kramerbooks & Afterwords, Inc.*).

The Supreme Court of Colorado similarly quashed a search warrant served upon a local independent bookstore that sought records showing a customer's bookstore purchases. The court held that the Colorado state constitution "requires that the government, when it seeks to use a search warrant to discover customer book purchase records from an innocent, third party bookstore, must demonstrate that it has a compelling need for the information sought" and that "the court must then balance the law enforcement officials' need for the bookstore record against the harm caused to constitutional interests by execution of the search warrant" (*Tattered Cover, Inc. v. City of Thornton*).

A local prosecutor in Decatur, Texas, served a subpoena on the local library that sought the personal information of all persons who had borrowed books on child bearing when an infant was abandoned. As in the bookstore cases, the judge applied a balancing test. He held that the subpoena represented an intrusion into library users' privacy that could be justified only when there is a compelling government objective that cannot be achieved by less intrusive means. The judge quashed the subpoena after the prosecutor could not prove the existence of a compelling need for the library records (*Decatur Public Library v. District Att'y of Wise County*).

Both public and private institutions can ask a court to quash or set aside a subpoena or court order seeking individuals' library records if the institution believes producing the records will inhibit the exercise of the First Amendment right to read and receive information. Although the First Amendment is not an absolute shield, judicial review of subpoenas helps ensure that readers' privacy is not infringed without good cause and justification.

Additional Resources

Decatur Public Library v. District Att'y of Wise County, No. 90-05-192, 271st Judicial Court (Texas, 1990)
In re Grand Jury Subpoena to Kramerbooks & Afterwords, Inc., 26 Med. L. Rptr. 1599 (D.D.C. 1998)
Lamont v. Postmaster General, 381 U.S. 301 (1965)
McIntyre v. Ohio Elections Commission, 514 U.S. 334 (1995)
Stanley v. Georgia, 394 U.S. 557 (1969)
Tattered Cover, Inc. v. City of Thornton, 44 P.3d 1044 (Colo. 2002)

the Fifth from self-incrimination. Historic cases such as *Griswold v. Connecticut* (381 U.S. 479 [1965]) implicitly protect privacy by acknowledging a "zone of privacy" that the government cannot permeate. *Whalen v. Roe* (429 U.S. 389 [1977]) applied directly to information privacy but fell short of addressing the problem comprehensively. This case ruled on a New York State statute requiring that records be kept of persons for whom addictive medicines were prescribed. The court acknowledged that New York had a serious burden of responsibility not to disclose this information. In so doing, the court extended the zone of privacy to the "individual interest in avoiding disclosure of personal matters." (Previously it had defined the zone of privacy only as a protection of the individual's right to privacy to make certain decisions about him- or herself.) The court did not go as far as the plaintiffs had wished; that is, the court did not address the plaintiffs' fear of losing control over their personal information. (Just as the existence of a law can dampen free speech even if a person is not prosecuted, so a law requiring that the state record a person's name might chill his or her getting a prescription filled.) One presumes that a case will arise to extend or clarify current precedent.[7]

PRIVACY AND TECHNOLOGY

Libraries were addressing user privacy concerns long before computers entered the scene. Most state library confidentiality laws were passed in the 1970s or earlier. Electronic integrated library systems and computer terminals with Internet access added enough complexity to the issue so that in 2001 the ALA Intellectual Freedom Committee established a standing privacy subcommittee. But in many ways the library professional ethics about privacy remain the same, regardless of technology.[8]

Yet there is no question that electronic technology and the Internet have rendered it easier to invade personal privacy than before, and the questions have been reframed as a result. Digital technology expert Esther Dyson has used the word "friction" to describe the encounter between the Internet and traditional privacy concerns. Nobody knows this better than computer security analysts themselves, who have worked for years in this arena and know what is possible in the digital age. A revealing and expert book is *Privacy Lost: How Technology Is Endangering Your Privacy* by David H. Holtzman, a former military cryptographer, intelligence analyst, and security consultant for corporations. His blog, at www.GlobalPOV.com, shows how technology and society affect each other.[9]

PRIVACY IN HIGHER EDUCATION AND ACADEMIC LIBRARIES

The U.S. public is experiencing firsthand what librarians and higher education have been grappling with for years now—how to balance freedom of expression, especially the right of access to information, with the right to privacy on a college campus and in an academic library. We want the freedom to read anything we wish and to have access to our government's information so that we can be participants in a democratic society. But what happens when the government decides that some information needs to be withheld, for the public good? What happens when a government decides that information surveillance via such efficient means as a national identity card or wiretapping provides a social good more important than the loss of one's personal privacy?

Academe now has any number of privacy laws to contend with, from the admissions office to the athletic department. Librarians would be wise to link their privacy issues to those affecting higher education as a whole—the Family Educational Rights and Privacy Act (FERPA), for example (see below). Campus review procedures for conducting research on human subjects, for example, are a common ground shared by the library when it seeks to protect user study participants.

On college and university campuses, many faculty assume they have the right to monitor student coursework, so they are often puzzled when the library refuses to let them check reserve lists to see which students are reading what. Indeed, some policy-makers think that privacy is dead and that we should, instead, put our energy into creating a truly transparent society and hold privacy violators accountable. This is the perspective of such thinkers as David Brin in his book *The Transparent Society: Will Technology Force Us to Choose between Privacy and Freedom?*[10] Daniel Solove, author of *The Digital Person,* disagrees:

> Affording mutuality of access to information will do little to empower ordinary individuals. The reason is that information is much more of an effective tool in the hands of a large bureaucracy. Information is not the key to power in the Information Age—knowledge is. Information consists of raw facts. Knowledge is information that has been sifted, sorted, and analyzed. The mere possession of information does not give one power; it is the ability to process that information and the capability to use the data that matter. In order to solve the problem, a transparent society would have to make each individual as competent as bureaucratic organizations in processing information into knowledge.[11]

For academic libraries, privacy concerns are complicated by the fact that many users simply do not care about, or are unaware of, the privacy implications of their daily library transactions. Millennials—most current undergraduates, in other words—are not as concerned about personal privacy as their parents' generation:

The youngest adult generation grew up with computers. They are adept at using digital cameras, cell phones, and MP3 players and are expert at texting, downloading the latest great song, blogging, and emailing, although they prefer instant messaging and use it most often when communicating with friends. When traveling in the third world, they can be found staring stupidly at dial telephones, pushing the holes repeatedly and shaking the handset. They trust computers more than they trust people.[12]

An important report released in late 2007 is OCLC's *Sharing, Privacy and Trust in Our Networked World*.[13] Regardless of whether one agrees with the findings, they should be read before the library community goes much further in deciding what actions to take in regard to privacy. The report finds that the younger generation behaves as if privacy is not a concern; they take no personal privacy precautions when using social networking. At the same time, they report that privacy is important to them. Young Americans trust that their privacy is secure. U.S. library directors were polled separately from the general public. Directors assume that library patrons care more about privacy than they actually report in the survey. Indeed, library directors care more about privacy than the general public; they implement far more privacy protections in their libraries than the public perceives are there.

This survey of 511 college students in countries including the United States also reports that use of digital communications is higher than that of the general public. In 2007, 56 percent had used a social networking site such as MySpace or Facebook, and 69 percent of those shared photos or videos. Almost 80 percent had given their first name, 65 percent their last name, and 75 percent their birthday. In terms of browsing and searching activities, only 15–20 percent believed that when they check out a book that information is private. In terms of trust, 31 percent of college students "trusted" those people they meet in person. This is almost double the percentage for social media or social networking sites. Of those students who have used a library website, between 60 and 70 percent thought it important to keep their personal information private. Many students do not believe it is the library's function to sponsor social networking sites. The OCLC survey results suggest that students are willing to make a privacy trade-off: they would rather sacrifice some personal privacy than give up social networking.

Their elders are far less trusting of the networked world—and arguably with good reason. Academic institutions hire legal counsel to prevent risky situations and lawsuits. The recent threats from the recording and motion picture industries to sue students for downloading music and movies, and the use of MySpace for sexual exploitation, encourage colleges to protect themselves from liability and ensure a risk-free learning community for young adults. Private institutions in most states have no mandate to follow the state laws on confidentiality of library records. As we have learned from the current controversy over the Communications Assistance for Law Enforcement Act (CALEA), some campuses have decided it is easier to lock down computer resources than to deal with the murky FCC policy process. Librarians are in a challenging situation, indeed. The existence of professional ethics to protect the privacy of library users sometimes gets lost in the campus aversion to risk.

This situation is further complicated by the fact that many privacy issues emerge from campus IT departments. These very professional colleagues—often the library's closest allies—are not always well versed in library professional values. Indeed, for many years they had their own "bill of rights and responsibilities." Professional organizations such as EDUCAUSE often have a very different take on privacy and may lean toward protecting campus electronic resources rather than promoting open access (although in recent years this stance has shifted dramatically).

The library profession will always want to "push the envelope" toward providing access to as much information as possible. The library profession is thus concerned about the increasingly restricted intellectual property laws and the First Amendment/privacy issues affecting campus technology. And, indeed, some of the biggest supporters of privacy come from the IT community.

But this clash of IT and library cultures is still a problem, and many campuses have addressed it directly via retreats or special staff development training. Library directors should always consult with IT departments about library policies; better yet, the two units should collaborate to develop campuswide privacy policies. Campus law school faculty can be invaluable committee members or advisors for such policy writing or review.

OVERARCHING PRINCIPLES, TOOLS, AND THINGS TO KNOW ABOUT PRIVACY IN ACADEMIC LIBRARIES

Students, faculty, and administration—and even some library colleagues—may not be familiar with library privacy issues. The OCLC privacy research cited earlier shows that only 4.5 percent of the public's concerns about privacy rights focus on library/reading privacy issues. The highest concerns were related to identity theft and the fraudulent use of credit cards. It is unclear from the OCLC report whether lack of concern about library privacy reflects lack of awareness or lack of concern. Although academic colleagues are almost certainly more knowledgeable about privacy issues than the general public, librarians should assume nothing and be prepared to present their case. Faculty and administrators frequently do not understand intuitively the link between broad campus privacy mandates (e.g., FERPA) and the confidentiality of library transactions. Once librarians convey this information—and it is important that librarians have a place at the proverbial table for communicating such information—there is usually buy-in at higher administrative levels.

Important Laws

State Library Confidentiality Statutes

Confidentiality statutes exist in forty-eight of fifty states, and these statutes vary a great deal.[14] Some laws protect library users in private institutions. Some do not protect any library users in any type of academic library. Some protect reference transactions, some only circulation transactions. State library organizations generally play a key watchdog role regarding their state statutes. In many states there has been an ongoing legislative effort to revise existing privacy laws to be consistent with the USA PATRIOT Act—thus making it easier for the government to compromise individual privacy rights in the interest of state security.

Conflicts may arise in special collections departments, where circulation records are often held in perpetuity in case a book is vandalized and the last user must be traced. These retrospective records are obviously sensitive; they should be retained only under lock and key and referred to only in the case of a legal investigation.

FERPA and Other Higher-Education Privacy Legislation

Most campuses are subject to FERPA and other federal privacy laws to protect the privacy of student records. The Council on Law in Higher Education's website

Library Confidentiality Statutes

Court decisions are not the only means of protecting the privacy of library users' records. Both Congress and state legislatures may enact specific statutes that recognize or extend privacy rights. Forty-eight states and the District of Columbia have adopted laws that specifically recognize the confidentiality of library records.

The substance of these statutes differs from state to state. Most declare library circulation records to be confidential and not subject to disclosure under the state's open records law or freedom of information legislation. Many states choose to extend additional protection to library records by imposing a duty on the library to protect user records from disclosure and limiting the circumstances under which a library may release records to third parties or law enforcement officers. For example, many state library confidentiality laws require service of a court order before a library can disclose records to law enforcement officers.

Library confidentiality laws may not apply to every library in a state or may except some users from full coverage of the law. For example, some state laws do not apply to private libraries; some exclude school libraries and academic libraries. A few state laws contain exceptions that permit parents of minor children to examine their children's library records. Other states choose to protect the confidentiality of all library users' records, without regard to the status of the library user or the funding, ownership, or control of the library.

State library confidentiality laws should be recognized and included in library policy whenever they are applicable to the library and its users. For private institutions, library confidentiality laws can serve as public policy exemplars that can provide a rationale and basis for the institutions' own policies protecting the confidentiality of library records.

Additional Resources

State Privacy Laws regarding Library Records: www.ala.org/ala/aboutala/offices/oif/ifgroups/stateifcchairs/stateifcinaction/stateprivacy.cfm (www.clhe.org) reviews all relevant laws and how they relate to each other. Librarians are responsible for keeping current with all these laws—to make sure they do not clash with library privacy policy and to notify campus when they do.

FERPA, enacted in 1974, guarantees the privacy of student records. Also known as the Buckley Amendment, FERPA prohibits employees of educational institutions from divulging information about student grades or behavior and from posting schoolwork on a bulletin board with a grade. If the child is a minor, this information can be divulged to a parent or guardian. When a student is eighteen or is enrolled in an institution beyond high school level, the rights transfer to the student. Academic librarians should point to FERPA as an example of the trend in higher education to keep student records private. This is why, for example, faculty should not monitor what individual students are reading and why libraries do not divulge circulation records of any kind—including reserves.

The USA PATRIOT Act of 2001 and 2006

> Librarians do not want to aid terrorists. One of us . . . had actually lost a friend on one of the planes that crashed into the World Trade Center. All four of us were deeply affected by the September 11 attacks, and none of us wanted any further harm to come to our country or its citizens. But we did not feel we would be helping the country or making anyone safer by throwing out the Constitution either. (George Christian, testimony to the U.S. Senate)[15]

Of all recent antiterrorism and privacy-related legislation, the USA PATRIOT Act has had the most powerful impact on library procedures, policies, and services.

USA PATRIOT Act is the acronym for "Uniting and Strengthening America by Providing Appropriate Tools Required to Intercept and Obstruct Terrorism" Act:

Family Educational Rights and Privacy Act

The Family Educational Rights and Privacy Act controls disclosure of a student's educational records and information. It requires educational institutions to adopt policies that permit students to inspect and correct their educational records. It also prohibits disclosure of a student's records without the student's written permission.

The Family Policy Compliance Office (FPCO), a part of the U.S. Department of Education, is the federal office charged with overseeing and enforcing FERPA. It frequently offers guidance and technical assistance to educational institutions by providing information on the law's application to particular circumstances.

Any record maintained by an educational institution directly related to a student, in any format, that allows the student to be identified from the information contained in it is considered an "educational record" by the FPCO. Analysts within FPCO have issued guidance stating that library circulation records and similar records maintained by a university library are "educational records" under FERPA.

Though FERPA generally requires institutions to protect the privacy of educational records, it contains many exceptions that allow disclosure of a student's educational records without the student's consent or permission. For example, FERPA permits educational institutions to release information contained in a student's records to any school official who has a "legitimate educational interest" in the records; to appropriate public officials in health and safety emergencies; and to courts and law enforcement agencies in response to a judicial order or lawfully issued subpoena. FERPA also permits educational institutions to disclose information about international students to the Department of Homeland Security and the Immigration and Customs Enforcement Bureau. In addition, colleges and universities may disclose records and information to the parents of adult students if the student is a tax dependent or is under twenty-one and has violated any law or regulation concerning the illegal use of drugs or alcohol.

FERPA thus permits disclosure when state library confidentiality statutes and professional ethics would otherwise prohibit the disclosure of library records. FERPA, however, does not require the institution to disclose records under these circumstances, nor does FERPA require institutions to create or maintain particular records. University and college libraries are therefore able to draw upon professional ethics and principles of academic freedom to craft policies that extend additional privacy protection to users' library records; adopt record retention policies that protect user confidentiality; and, where applicable, incorporate state law protections for library records.

Additional Resources

Code of Federal Regulations, Family educational rights and privacy, 34 C.F.R. Part 99

Family Educational Rights and Privacy Act, 20 U.S.C. 1232g

Family Policy Compliance Office, U.S. Department of Education: www.ed.gov/policy/gen/guid/fpco/index.html

Public Law 107-56, signed into law on October 26, 2001. A somewhat revised act was signed on March 9, 2006. Briefly, the legislation expanded more than fifteen existing statutes and added new surveillance and investigative powers so that law enforcement agencies could investigate suspected terrorism more easily. Section 215 allows the FBI to obtain library records of anyone, when the FBI shows "reasonable grounds" that the library records sought are relevant to an authorized investigation. The revised Section 215 does require a "particular" search, so that the original fear of "fishing expeditions" can be avoided. The reauthorized act also allows the librarian served with the order to consult with an attorney and to disclose the order to "other persons as permitted" by the director of the FBI. This provision is the so-called gag order.

It is entirely possible that a National Security Letter could be served on an academic library, at which point the library might be asked to surrender confidential circulation information otherwise protected by state law. It is up to the university or college librarian to make the campus administration aware of how the PATRIOT Act affects libraries and potentially compromises the privacy of campus community members. The ALA website provides the best information on the history and response of librarians to this act; see below.

The Library Connection, Inc., Case

What follows is a detailed description of the only major USA PATRIOT Act court case, a case that clearly demonstrates the serious impact of the law on libraries. If other libraries are served with a National Security Letter or search warrant, their attorneys and library leaders should review what happened in this case of Library Connection, Inc., and prepare accordingly. This could happen to any individual library or consortium, public or private, in the United States under the current provisions of the PATRIOT Act.

These details are derived from the testimony of George Christian, executive director of Library Connection, Inc., of Windsor, Connecticut, in his testimony on April 11, 2007, to the U.S. Senate Judiciary Subcommittee on the Constitution, Civil Rights and Property Rights. The Library Connection, Inc., is a consortium of twenty-seven Connecticut libraries.

> July 8, 2005: The FBI notified Library Connection via telephone that they would be served with a National Security Letter (hereafter NSL) to obtain information about a specific IP address registered to Library Connection and its use on February 15, 2005, for 45 minutes. There was no court order and no evidence that an independent judge had examined the FBI's request and evidence and found probable cause.

> Mr. Christian decided to oppose the effort, because he had kept current with library association and court efforts to declare the NSL aspect of the PATRIOT Act unconstitutional.

> July 13, 2005: Christian was served with the letter, which warned him he could not tell anyone that the consortium had been served (the gag order). Christian told the FBI agent that he had reason to believe that the NSL was unconstitutional, and he wanted to notify the Library Connection attorney. The FBI agent complied with that request. Christian called the attorney, who told him that the only way to contest compliance was to challenge the U.S. attorney general in court.

> July 14, 2005: Christian next called an emergency meeting of his Executive Committee and the attorney, because he did not think he could make such a decision alone using members' money on a case that could easily go to the

Law Enforcement and Requests for Library Records

Law enforcement officers frequently ask libraries and librarians to turn over information about library users or records reflecting users' reading habits or use of the Internet. Neither federal agents nor police officers are legally authorized to demand an individual's library records or confidential information without first providing some form of *judicial process*—a subpoena, a search warrant, or other legally enforceable order—to the library holding the records.

A *subpoena* is the most common means used to compel the production of library records. A subpoena is issued by a grand jury or court and is usually signed by the prosecuting attorney; sometimes the subpoena is signed by a judge. The subpoena identifies the records that are sought for the investigation and instructs the library or librarian to produce those records at a certain date, time, and place.

The librarian should carefully examine the subpoena with legal counsel to ensure that it was issued correctly and contains all required signatures, information, and notices. If the librarian or the library's legal counsel believes that the subpoena is unjustified for any reason or that compliance with the subpoena will hinder the exercise of First Amendment rights in the library, the library can file a motion to quash the subpoena before a court with jurisdiction over the investigation.

A *search warrant* is a court order that authorizes law enforcement officers to search for and seize particular items in a particular location. It is issued by a court and signed by a judge after a hearing to determine if "probable cause" exists—that is, good cause to believe the search will produce evidence of a crime. The police officer may serve the search warrant on the library at any time, and the library is required to permit the search for the items listed in the search warrant or to provide the officer with the items.

Since a search warrant authorizes the police to conduct the search without notice and without delay, there is little or no opportunity to challenge a search warrant in a court of law before the library is required to comply with the search warrant. The Supreme Court has ruled that the initial hearing to determine the existence of probable cause provides sufficient protection for individual civil rights, including First Amendment rights (*Zurcher v. Stanford Daily News*).

FISA orders are court orders authorized by the Foreign Intelligence Surveillance Act (FISA), as amended by Section 215 of the USA PATRIOT Act. FISA orders are issued by the Foreign Intelligence Surveillance Court (FISC) and authorize FBI agents to seize "any tangible thing," including documents, records, computer disks, and any other physical object, as long as the FBI agent alleges that the item is relevant to an ongoing investigation into terrorism or foreign espionage. Under Section 215, a party served with a FISA order is subject to an automatic nondisclosure order, or "gag order," that forbids recipients of a FISA order from disclosing to anyone that they have received a FISA order or that records have been turned over to the FBI. The USA

PATRIOT Act allows the recipient of a FISA order to challenge the order in the FISC, but the court will not quash a FISA order unless the court finds it "unlawful." The gag order may be challenged in the FISC one year after the service of the FISA order.

National Security Letters (NSLs) are specialized, written orders to turn over records that are issued by the FBI. Section 505 of the USA PATRIOT Act expanded the FBI's authority to utilize these orders to obtain certain types of records, including electronic communication records that may be held by a library providing Internet services. Like recipients of FISA orders, NSL recipients are subject to a nondisclosure order forbidding any recipient from disclosing the existence of the NSL or that records were turned over to the FBI.

The law authorizes the FBI to issue these orders without any judicial review or supervision by a court. Refusal to comply with the order or violating the nondisclosure order is a crime. A recipient of an NSL can, however, challenge the legality of an NSL and its accompanying gag order in a federal district court.

In 2004 and 2005, NSL recipients filed lawsuits challenging the constitutionality of NSL orders and the gag order that is automatically issued with NSLs. Though courts in each case initially ruled that the NSLs and gag orders were unconstitutional, the courts' decisions were mooted by the 2006 revision of the USA PATRIOT Act. When the courts were instructed to reexamine the constitutionality of NSLs in light of the revised law, the government prevented final review of the NSLs by withdrawing the orders.

A subsequent challenge to the NSL statute and the gag order in the federal district courts found the use of NSL unconstitutional. That decision is under review by the Second Circuit Court of Appeals.

All libraries, public or private, should have written policies and procedures for handling subpoenas, search warrants, and PATRIOT Act orders. Such written policies ensure that every request for records is handled in accordance with the law. Sample policies may be found on the ALA website.

Additional Resources

Confidentiality and Coping with Law Enforcement Inquiries: Guidelines for the Library and Its Staff: www.ala.org/ala/aboutala/offices/oif/ifissues/confidentiality.cfm

Gotham City Model Policy 1.1 and Gotham City Model Staff Directive 1.5 (same source as above)

Supreme Court. (Note that at this point, by holding this meeting, Christian was defying the NSL's gag order.) The group decided to oppose the NSL. Because of the way the computer network is configured, the only way the FBI could trace the path would be to find out who was using every terminal in one specific member library for that day. And, because five months later there was no way to trace who was using computers in the library on that day, the FBI would need to get information on all patrons of that library. The group concluded that that qualified as a "fishing expedition" and therefore they would oppose the effort. The group also decided to seek relief from the NSL gag order.

August 2005: The Executive Committee met with ACLU (American Civil Liberties Union) attorneys. They decided to seek an injunction "relieving Library Connection from complying with the NSL and to seek a broader ruling that the use of NSLs is unconstitutional. The Committee also decided to seek relief from the gag rules associated with NSLs in order to (1) allow the Executive Committee's actions to be presented to the full Board, and (2) to allow the fact that an NSL was served on a library organization to become part of the national debate over renewal of the PATRIOT Act."

August 2005: ACLU filed suit in federal district court in Bridgeport, Conn. Library Connection, Inc. was identified as "John Doe," so the case was *Doe v. Gonzales* (386 F. Supp. 2d 66 [D. Conn. 2005]; Alberto Gonzales was the U.S. attorney general at that time). Executive Committee members prepared affidavits to be filed with the suit. The Library Connection plaintiffs were not allowed in the courtroom for the hearing because they would then be identifiable. They had to watch the proceedings over closed-circuit television in the Hartford Federal Court Building.

Judge Hall ruled that a perpetual gag order was prior restraint and therefore unconstitutional. This ruling was immediately appealed by the U.S. Justice Department. Christian reveals in his testimony how personally frustrating and frightening a gag order is: "I knew that all the board members and all the member library directors knew of the case, and I suspected the Executive Committee and I had their approval. However, I had no idea whether the approval was unanimous, or whether there was a significant dissenting opinion. I felt terrible I could not let anyone know that the struggle was not depleting our capital reserves and putting the corporation at risk. I could not even tell our auditors that the corporation was engaged in a major lawsuit—a direct violation of my fiduciary responsibilities. I pride myself on my integrity and openness. . . . One of the John Does even had his son ask 'Dad, is the FBI after you?'"

November 6, 2005: Not surprisingly, bureaucracies have problems keeping secrets because of the enormous amount of paperwork and the number of people handling it. In this case, the plaintiffs' identity was accidentally identified on the court's website. At that point, the press discovered the case and the plaintiffs. Thus the front page of the *Washington Post* carried the story. Attorneys advised the plaintiffs not to make any comment at all. The plaintiffs were not allowed to share the experience with Congress, which was at that time debating the renewal of the PATRIOT Act.

November 2005: The Second Court of Appeals in New York heard the case, and the plaintiffs were allowed to be present, though they could not establish eye contact with each other or sit together. Christian: "Our attorneys filed more legal papers to try to lift the gag, and attached copies of the *New York Times* articles. The government claimed that all the press coverage revealing our names did not matter because (1) no one in Connecticut reads the *New York Times* and (2) surveys prove that 58 percent of the public disbelieves what they read in newspapers. To add to the absurdity, the government insisted that the copies of the news stories our attorneys had submitted remain under seal in court papers."

Because it appeared that Congress would vote on the act's renewal before the appellate court could rule, the Library Connection attorneys took the case to the Supreme Court, which was troubled but refused to lift the gag at that point.

March 9, 2006: President Bush signed the revised USA PATRIOT Act.

A few weeks later, the government decided that the Library Connection's silence was no longer necessary and told the Second Circuit that the FBI would lift the gag. The government tried to get Judge Hall's decision vacated as moot. The Second Circuit refused. Judge Cardamone of the Second Circuit: "A ban on speech and a shroud of secrecy in perpetuity are antithetical to democratic concepts and do not fit comfortably with the fundamental rights guaranteed American citizens. . . . Unending secrecy of actions taken by government officials may also serve as a cover for possible official misconduct and/or incompetence." The court then referred the rest of the case back to the district court, so that Justice Hall's original opinion about the unconstitutionality of the gag order is part of case law.

A few weeks later, the FBI abandoned the case.

May 31, 2006: The Library Connection held its first press conference. The *Hartford Courant* headline was "Librarians Shushed No More."

Every case between a library and the PATRIOT Act is likely to differ dramatically. For that reason, it is important to have written policies and staff training on the general principles. But it does help to read about how an actual confrontation played out. This chapter gives resources for writing your library's privacy policies and instructions on what to do if law enforcement officials visit your library.

CALEA

As this book goes to press, the FCC has not yet finalized its CALEA implementation guidelines. Librarians should consult the ALA website, specifically the Office for Information Technology, for the latest information on whether libraries are required to comply. The law is complex, and each library needs to examine its telecommunications configuration to determine compliance.[16] For the following discussion I relied on the legal analysis of Albert Gidari, partner of Perkins Coie of Seattle and a telecommunications specialist whose interpretations can be found on the ALA website.[17]

CALEA was passed by Congress in 1994. It requires telecommunications carriers to ensure that their equipment and services can conduct real-time electronic surveillance, without the knowledge of the person under surveillance. Simply put, phone companies must make it easy for law enforcement agencies to conduct wiretapping on phone lines. This law has now been extended to Internet service providers (ISPs).

How does this work technologically? Campuses need to know how they are connected to the Internet:

1. If an institution is connected from a commercial ISP that provides the "pipe" to the Internet *and* the campus router that directs traffic to it, then the ISP is required to comply with CALEA.
2. If an institution is connected from a commercial ISP that provides the "pipe" to the Internet but the institution owns the router that directs the traffic to it, then the institution must ensure that the router is compliant, but the campus network is still considered a "private network" and has no obligation. The requirements for the router in this case have not yet been established.
3. If the institution provides direct Internet access to the public at large, then the institution must be CALEA compliant.

What about "incidental use"—for example, campus alumni visitors, conference attendees on a campus other than their own, or the public wanting access to federal documents? Gidari states that "nothing in CALEA, in the FCC Order or the court decision defines a private user community, nor does anything require that a community of users be specifically identified through assignment of user IDs or another authentication system." Thus some campuses are allowing "incidental use" and are not mandating a system of user authentication. Others are mandating user authentication in all cases. The FCC has still not completed its regulations. Gidari has stated, in fact, that

some academic libraries permit access to the general public and indeed, in some instances, are required to do so by law. But such access will have no effect on whether or not an academic institution is a private network. The FCC excluded libraries from CALEA coverage whenever access was obtained from a third party. By definition, a private network does not provide access to the Internet. When an exempt academic library is part of an exempt private network, the obligation for CALEA compliance falls on the entity that provides the facilities that support connection to the Internet.

For example, on some campuses there is a campus network that includes the library computers. The campus network connects to the Internet through an ISP. This ISP is likely to be covered by CALEA and is required to comply; that is, the ISP must ensure that its equipment can be wiretapped easily, in real time, and must monitor traffic 24/7. *If* the ISP complies, then the campus network can in most cases be defined as a private network, because it is available only to those having access to the campus network through a password. Further, the FCC has suggested in footnotes and guidelines that library, hotel, and coffee shop use of the Internet is "incidental use" and is exempt from CALEA compliance. Thus, many campuses are declaring that they are private networks and thus exempt from CALEA.

The problem is this: Many libraries are open to the general public, who up until now have not been required (on some campuses, at least) to have a password (user authentication) to use the Internet. Further, libraries that are federal document depositories are required by law to be open to the public. Thus, libraries are caught between the regulations of the federal document depository system and the regulations regarding CALEA.

Depending on how much risk a campus decides to bear, libraries comply (or not) in different ways and degrees. Some are defining public use of their network as "incidental." Others are requiring that the public now be given guest passwords. Some are locking down their wireless networks so that only campus users have access. Some campuses with locked-down terminals are providing signage to guide government document users to terminals that can access only .mil or .gov sites.

ALA Resources for Policy Formulation

Privacy continues to be a major concern of the ALA's Office for Intellectual Freedom and Intellectual Freedom Committee. The ALA website should be consulted at least weekly for the latest privacy legislation, court decisions, and association initiatives. In addition, the *Intellectual Freedom Manual* provides a wealth of guidance on policy formulation. The recently announced "national conversation on privacy" will undoubtedly enrich librarians' knowledge and resources for enacting good privacy policies.

Part 3, chapter 5 of the *Intellectual Freedom Manual,* 7th ed. (along with www .ala.org/ala/aboutala/offices/oif/ifissues/privacyconfidentiality.cfm) provides the philosophical underpinnings for ALA's stance on confidentiality, privacy, and government intimidation:

5.1 Policy on Confidentiality of Library Records

ALA recommends that all library directors adopt a confidentiality policy, train their staff, and resist government attempts to compromise that policy (*Intellectual Freedom Manual,* 293–94).

5.2 Suggested Procedures for Implementing "Policy on Confidentiality of Library Records"

This supplementary document suggests ways for the library to work with its attorney and staff to implement a practical policy on confidentiality of library records (*Intellectual Freedom Manual,* 300–301).

5.3 Confidentiality and Coping with Law Enforcement Inquiries: Guidelines for the Library and Its Staff

These guidelines, among the most important in the entire seventh edition, include a useful listing of all ALA policies to date relating to privacy (*Intellectual Freedom Manual*, 304–13).

5.4 Policy concerning Confidentiality of Personally Identifiable Information and Library Users

A ringing reminder that libraries' protection of the privacy of their users is one of the profession's highest values, even in the face of government intimidation (*Intellectual Freedom Manual*, 314–15).

5.5 Guidelines for Developing a Library Privacy Policy Toolkit

Do not start from scratch! Here is a template that will certainly work for academic library privacy policy packets (*Intellectual Freedom Manual*, 319–32).

Other Helpful Organizations

- American Civil Liberties Union: www.aclu.org, especially the "Privacy and Technology" Project
- EDUCAUSE: www.educause.edu
- Electronic Frontier Foundation: www.eff.org
- EPIC (Electronic Privacy Information Center): www.epic.org
- First Amendment Center: www.firstamendmentcenter.org
- Privacy International: www.privacyinternational.org

Privacy Audits

One of the most valuable activities a library director can spearhead is a campuswide *privacy audit,* conducted with the IT and other concerned departments. A privacy audit is an excellent way to share values and ensure consistency of campus policies. Chances are that they are inconsistent; campus technology growth has been incremental, with different departments adopting different policies over time. The following are but a few examples of the kinds of library activities and records that should be subject to a privacy audit.

Transaction Logs on Computer Workstations

The library or IT services should have a written policy on retention of transaction logs. If the FBI investigates and finds that logs have been destroyed systematically according to a written records retention policy, that is generally acceptable. If, however, the logs have been destroyed erratically, without a consistent written policy, the FBI could question whether the records were destroyed selectively. The best rule of thumb is to keep logs only as long as they are needed for the operational needs of the college or university.

In a February 2007 issue of the *Chronicle of Higher Education,* attorney Douglas Seaver urges that higher education be prepared to provide more electronic information to opponents in court, because of new federal amendments to civil procedures in December 2006. It is important for librarians to understand and be part of the institution's discussion of these issues and development of the policy so that the institution respects library privacy laws and policies. Electronic discovery is an increasingly important component in litigation. If IT services or any other technology unit holds electronic library records, or if records are held in a consortium, librarians should know the retention policy. Seaver concludes:

> What is clear is that all legal counsel involved in litigation will now have to become familiar with their clients' computer systems and programs, policies for document retention and destruction, computer processes for harvesting relevant data from vast stores of electronically stored information, and ways to negotiate the means and methods of producing electronically stored information with opposing counsel. . . . people who work on campus . . . should understand that their electronic documents may become evidence in litigation, and that, as a result, they should be judicious in the information that they create, receive, retain, or send. They must also be ready to preserve and protect electronically stored information once they learn that litigation against the institution is likely or has begun.[18]

Librarians should keep in mind that, when it comes to the current federal initiatives to expand wiretapping powers in the name of national security, campus administrations and their attorneys are increasingly risk averse and not necessarily receptive to those campus units adamant about protecting privacy rights. Librarians and others dedicated to protecting the privacy rights of patrons must be able to justify their stance with supporting laws and court decisions.

Circulation Records

The library should keep circulation records only as long as they are needed for the management and workflow needs of the library. In most cases, once a book has been returned, the link between the book title and the name of the individual borrower can be broken. This should be done on a regular basis, consistently, and according to written policy.

User Surveys or Focus Groups

Surveys are often a useful way to measure and assess effectiveness of particular services or search algorithms. There is no problem with such surveys, as long as personally identifiable information is not included. When the use of such personal information is necessary, one must usually receive permission from the campus human subjects review board and also the permission of the individual participants in the survey.

Confidentiality of Reference Transactions

It is so easy to be casual about reference transactions. And yet in some states the confidentiality law includes the privacy rights of a reference interview. It is good professional practice, in any case, to conduct such interviews in as private a manner as possible. Also, when asking library reference colleagues for assistance in answering a tough question, it is good practice to confer with colleagues without mentioning the name of the patron seeking the information.

Confidentiality in Special Collections: Some Special Considerations

Special collections departments often keep circulation records for an extended period of time because the materials are often unique and must be checked for damage or theft of pages. Such records should be kept in a secure place with only authorized librarians permitted to consult them, unless served with a court-ordered subpoena, search warrant, or National Security Letter.

Tracking Legislation such as the USA PATRIOT Act and CALEA

Librarians must keep track of congressional legislation, which is likely to continue advocating broader government power to track terrorists or terrorist sympathizers.

Technology such as RFID and Course Management Software

RFID (radio frequency identification) is but one of many technologies librarians need to understand before they purchase or adopt it. In many cases, technologies have been developed without consultation with librarians, or developed for a different purpose and then adopted by libraries with no thought given to the privacy implications. One such technology is RFID, which involves tags that contain information. The tags were originally used by industry to track shipments of goods from manufacturer to warehouse to retail stores—and then sometimes to the home. This technology helps prevent theft and track shipments.

The problem comes when RFID is applied to library circulation systems, through the law of unintended consequences. An RFID tag is placed in a book. Then a patron can check out the book with a wand. This has bad and good implications. The good is that a patron checks out a book in total privacy—not even a circulation staff member handles the transaction. But, depending on what information is stored on the tag and how much range the signal tracking system has—the book can then be tracked from the library to the home of the patron. So, theoretically, RFID could be used by police to track a title to one's home. Some nongovernmental organizations are opposed to RFID applications: Electronic Frontier Foundation was part of the pressure group that prevented San Francisco Public Library from implementing the technology. Others take the approach that libraries can implement it if they know how it works and limit the frequency and information stored on the tag. That is the approach ALA took in its policy on RFID, as outlined at www.ala.org/ala/aboutala/offices/oif/ifissues/confidentiality.cfm.

CASE STUDY 1

"Faculty members have a right to know whether their students are doing the required readings. I want to see the records of who is reading the reserve material for my class."

Professor Jones assigns a percentage of each student's course grade on the basis of the student's reading of reserve materials. Jones can use the course management system (Blackboard is an example of such a system) to track which readings a particular student has accessed and the length of time spent reading. The library's e-reserve system does not have this tracking capability, and the circulation of materials on the "traditional" print shelves is kept confidential. However, the course management system is operated by the IT department, which does not have a confidentiality policy. The university librarian asks that IT and the faculty work together with the library to protect student privacy. The university is private and its state confidentiality statute does not cover academic libraries or private libraries in any case.

One approach to this and similar cases is to pose some key questions:

- Is there an all-encompassing campuswide document defining student privacy rights?
- Does the particular state confidentiality statute apply to this academic library?
- Does the content on the course management system belong to the library? Is the operation of the course management system under the library's purview?
- Does the course management system have blocking capabilities for breaking the link to personally identifiable information?

If the library is subject to its state's confidentiality statute or has adopted it in principle, it appears obvious that, regardless of the delivery system of the library-owned materials, library patron privacy prevails. The entire campus must be made aware of this all-important principle, especially if the library-owned materials are downloaded into a system not under the library's control.

Some faculty may initially feel they have an absolute right to monitor what students are reading. Once the library explains that this "right" abridges academic freedom and other student confidentiality statutes, faculty often change their minds. Other arguments that might help clarify the library privacy policy:

- If faculty are not allowed to see what students have checked out of the library on traditional reserve or through regular circulation, why should they be able to see what students are reading on the course management system?
- The fact that a student has logged onto the course management site does not prove that he or she has read the materials.

- A student might well own the assigned books or borrow them from a classmate. It would be unfair for a professor to make assumptions on the basis of course management system records.

A word on selection of course management systems. Some course management systems allow for local control of the monitoring features. The library must be a participant in the adoption or purchase of any campus software with privacy implications. When your campus purchases a courseware management system, be sure to include privacy criteria in the specifications or request for proposal. Remember that quite often electronic software includes "bells and whistles" not requested or needed by the purchaser. Developers may have included features just because they were able to build them. Librarians and library associations must become better at anticipating product development and include privacy specifications from the very beginning. In the 1980s and 1990s, when integrated library system vendors developed their products, librarians communicated circulation privacy specifications during the development phase and all the major vendors included privacy features as a result. If your course management software does not have a switch, then librarians should (1) encourage faculty not to utilize this feature and (2) make sure students are aware of this potential invasion of their personal privacy. ■

"Who's got this book checked out? I'll go over to his dorm and get it and then return it to him when I'm done with it."

Ben, a student working at the circulation desk, is asked by Melanie to find out who has checked out a particular book Melanie needs to complete her term paper due in two days. Ben searches the online circulation record, calls the person who has checked out the book, and asks if Melanie can borrow it for a few hours. Melanie has offered to pick up and return the book, along with a pizza as a bonus.

Many state confidentiality statutes prohibit academic libraries from revealing circulation records. Libraries should make sure they are applying the same patron privacy protection to any type of library information—including interlibrary loan, reserves, and circulation of newspapers from behind a service counter. Even if the state confidentiality statute does not apply in your situation, many academic libraries (both private and public) do protect patron privacy on the basis of ALA's Code of Ethics and Library Bill of Rights. In the case of a manual reserve system, cross out the names on the circulation card with a very dark marker.

Training of student workers is crucial to any implementation of library privacy policies. Students are subject to peer pressure, and this leads to the temptation not only to reveal circulation records but also to delete fines. Written training materials, policies, and copies of applicable laws are important tools for helping student workers resist peer pressure. In addition, circulation desk personnel should be given access only to those circulation system functions necessary for doing their jobs.

Confidentiality of circulation records is problematic on small college campuses, where all students, faculty, and librarians know each other and a culture of informality suggests there is no need to enforce privacy policies. One strategy to tackle such informality is to invoke community values. Explain to students and faculty that, when books are circulated informally, the borrower often loses or damages the book. The wrong person might get billed for the loss and blocked from graduation or other campus privileges.

I know of a colleague serving on a promotion and tenure committee at another university who was assigned by that committee to investigate what a tenure candidate had checked out of the campus library over the previous three years. The committee used circulation records as a means to measure "intellectual curiosity." Such information can also be used to investigate plagiarism cases. Such practices are certainly unethical, inaccurate, incomplete from an evidentiary standpoint, and perhaps illegal.

Remember, too, that it is easy to overlook the importance of interlibrary loan privacy. Paper notification of such loan arrivals should be mailed in an envelope or via private e-mail, and books should be distributed via a numerical system. Flags with patron names prominently displayed should be avoided. ■

"Does anybody know the answer to Stephanie's question?"

The reference librarian on duty is approached at the desk by a student, Stephanie, who poses a complex ethical question about abortion—not this librarian's forte. The librarian thus sends out an e-mail message to her reference department colleagues to solicit further expertise.

In some states, reference questions are protected by privacy statutes. It is wise to assume that all library transactions between a patron and an information provider are confidential. It is certainly prudent in this case to ask the assistance of colleagues, but it is unnecessary to reveal the name of the patron asking the question. This cautionary best practice can be crucial for sensitive areas of research or when providing reference assistance to a faculty member who might well be in competition with others for publishing a discovery first or receiving appropriate credit for a particular piece of research.

A researcher once asked me whether others were working on the same topic he was (this often happens in special collections services). In such a case the librarian can contact others working on the topic to see if they are willing to be contacted, and then an arrangement can be made under mutual agreement. ■

"I am Agent Jones from the FBI. I need to check the library records to see who has been interested in anthrax."

An FBI agent approaches a student worker at the desk of the College of Veterinary Medicine library and asks for circulation and database search records for all transactions on the topic of anthrax.

I hope that you are reading this case study in a moment of relative calm. However, if a law enforcement officer is in your library right now and you have no written procedures, you should either call your campus attorney or the ALA Office for Intellectual Freedom. If you have been served with a search warrant under the USA PATRIOT Act antiterrorism provisions, your conversation with ALA should be simple: "I need legal advice." You should not reveal the existence of a search warrant.

Every single student worker, staff member, volunteer, and librarian needs to be familiar with the library's procedures in case of a visit by a law enforcement officer. Such procedures should be *written,* discussed with all staff, and approved by the campus administration including legal counsel. Elsewhere in this chapter are guidelines from the *Intellectual Freedom Manual* on what to include. The ALA website always includes up-to-date advice for such procedures.

Remember that in all cases of a visit by a law enforcement officer, the library and its college or university has rights and a certain amount of time for an appropriate response. It is always advisable to take a deep breath and call the library director or campus attorney before surrendering any library records. Law enforcement is required to present certain legal documents, such as a subpoena or search warrant, and the frontline desk responder is always advised to check with a supervisor before taking any action.

Be prepared for a visit by a law enforcement officer with the following materials and plans established beforehand:

At each service point, keep phone numbers and contact information for the library director or designee, campus attorney, and ALA Office for Intellectual Freedom, with numbered steps of whom to call in order—including instructions for evenings and weekends. Generally, it is preferable to call the library director or designee first to start the chain of action regarding the response to the visit. It is important to know ahead of time at what point to phone the campus police rather than the community police. Remember that a student worker or staff member unfamiliar with the procedures might be the officer's first contact. Because these situations happen so infrequently and can be frightening, a script might be helpful.

Prepare a folder to present to the law enforcement officer, containing any relevant state statutes or other legal information. It might also include links to or printed versions of library policies and procedures. Such information conveys the expertise and experience of the library in dealing with law enforcement inquiries and makes misunderstandings and miscommunication less likely.

Local policies should include your data retention schedules, a system for obtaining operational records within your institution, and a service continuity plan in case workstations, servers, or backups are removed. For templates on privacy policies, see the ALA website for the latest suggestions.

Law enforcement officers must present some type of legal document in order to obtain access to library property or confidential information. This might be a National Security Letter, a search warrant, or a court-ordered subpoena. The campus legal counsel should assist you in determining if such papers are in order before the campus surrenders any documents. Since library searches began under the authorization of the USA PATRIOT Act, ALA has done yeoman's duty on assembling and creating boilerplate materials for library policies and procedures in the event of law enforcement inquiries. Check the ALA website for such examples as the Colorado Association of Libraries set of guidelines (www.cal-webs.org), which can be adapted for use in most academic libraries. All types of law enforcement inquiries are covered in this single concise document.

Document any locally incurred costs. The PATRIOT Act does provide for reimbursement of costs incurred in extensive data retrieval.

When allowed by law and on the advice of your legal counsel, talk with the local press about your experience and report it to ALA's Washington, D.C., office. ■

NOTES

1. "The Future of Privacy: Can We Safeguard Our Information in a High-Tech, Insecure World?" the theme issue of *Scientific American,* September 2008.
2. The Federal Trade Commission website is filled with useful information about identity theft: www.ftc.gov.
3. See the ALA press release at www.ala.org/ala/newspresscenter/news/pressreleases2008/may2008/soros.cfm.
4. *Intellectual Freedom Manual,* 7th ed. (Chicago: American Library Association, 2006), 402.
5. M. Ethan Katsch, *Law in a Digital World* (New York: Oxford University Press, 1995), 234.
6. Samuel D. Warren and Louis D. Brandeis, "The Right to Privacy," 4 *Harvard Law Review* 193 (1890).
7. I acknowledge this analysis from Daniel Solove, *The Digital Person: Technology and Privacy in the Information Age* (New York: New York University Press, 2004), 64–65.
8. Esther Dyson, "How Loss of Privacy May Mean Loss of Security," *Scientific American,* September 2008, 90–95.
9. David H. Holtzman, *Privacy Lost: How Technology Is Endangering Your Privacy* (San Francisco: Jossey-Bass, 2006).
10. David Brin, *The Transparent Society: Will Technology Force Us to Choose between Privacy and Freedom?* (New York: Basic Books, 1999).
11. Solove, *Digital Person,* 73–74.
12. Holtzman, *Privacy Lost,* 144–45.
13. OCLC, *Sharing, Privacy and Trust in Our Networked World* (Dublin, Ohio: OCLC, 2007). Available at no cost as a PDF file: www.oclc.org/us/en/reports/sharing/default.htm.
14. ALA maintains a current listing of "State Privacy Laws regarding Library Records": www.ala.org/ala/aboutala/offices/oif/ifgroups/stateifcchairs/stateifcinaction/stateprivacy.cfm.
15. George Christian, Testimony for the Record to the Senate Judiciary Subcommittee on the Constitution, Civil Rights and Property Rights, Hearing, April 11, 2007, on behalf of the American Library Association. Quotations in the following review of the case are from a printout of the testimony from the ALA.

16. See *Scientific American,* September 2008, for an excellent and understandable presentation of the technological issues.
17. Albert Gidari, "Communications Assistance for Law Enforcement Act ('CALEA') and Private Networks in Academia," and "Libraries Are Exempt from CALEA Wiretap Obligations," www.ala.org/ala/aboutala/offices/wo/woissues/techinttele/calea.cfm.
18. Douglas F. Seaver, "The New Legal Advice: Don't Press 'Delete,'" *Chronicle of Higher Education,* February 16, 2007, B12–13.

Appendix

ALA Intellectual Freedom Documents

Code of Ethics of the American Library Association

As members of the American Library Association, we recognize the importance of codifying and making known to the profession and to the general public the ethical principles that guide the work of librarians, other professionals providing information services, library trustees and library staffs.

Ethical dilemmas occur when values are in conflict. The American Library Association Code of Ethics states the values to which we are committed, and embodies the ethical responsibilities of the profession in this changing information environment.

We significantly influence or control the selection, organization, preservation, and dissemination of information. In a political system grounded in an informed citizenry, we are members of a profession explicitly committed to intellectual freedom and the freedom of access to information. We have a special obligation to ensure the free flow of information and ideas to present and future generations.

The principles of this Code are expressed in broad statements to guide ethical decision making. These statements provide a framework; they cannot and do not dictate conduct to cover particular situations.

I. We provide the highest level of service to all library users through appropriate and usefully organized resources; equitable service policies; equitable access; and accurate, unbiased, and courteous responses to all requests.

II. We uphold the principles of intellectual freedom and resist all efforts to censor library resources.

III. We protect each library user's right to privacy and confidentiality with respect to information sought or received and resources consulted, borrowed, acquired or transmitted.

IV. We respect intellectual property rights and advocate balance between the interests of information users and rights holders.

V. We treat co-workers and other colleagues with respect, fairness, and good faith, and advocate conditions of employment that safeguard the rights and welfare of all employees of our institutions.

VI. We do not advance private interests at the expense of library users, colleagues, or our employing institutions.

VII. We distinguish between our personal convictions and professional duties and do not allow our personal beliefs to interfere with fair representation of the aims of our institutions or the provision of access to their information resources.

VIII. We strive for excellence in the profession by maintaining and enhancing our own knowledge and skills, by encouraging the professional development of co-workers, and by fostering the aspirations of potential members of the profession.

Adopted June 28, 1997, by the ALA Council; amended January 22, 2008.

The Library Bill of Rights

The American Library Association affirms that all libraries are forums for information and ideas, and that the following basic policies should guide their services.

I. Books and other library resources should be provided for the interest, information, and enlightenment of all people of the community the library serves. Materials should not be excluded because of the origin, background, or views of those contributing to their creation.

II. Libraries should provide materials and information presenting all points of view on current and historical issues. Materials should not be proscribed or removed because of partisan or doctrinal disapproval.

III. Libraries should challenge censorship in the fulfillment of their responsibility to provide information and enlightenment.

IV. Libraries should cooperate with all persons and groups concerned with resisting abridgment of free expression and free access to ideas.

V. A person's right to use a library should not be denied or abridged because of origin, age, background, or views.

VI. Libraries which make exhibit spaces and meeting rooms available to the public they serve should make such facilities available on an equitable basis, regardless of the beliefs or affiliations of individuals or groups requesting their use.

Adopted June 18, 1948. Amended February 2, 1961, and January 23, 1980, inclusion of "age" reaffirmed January 23, 1996, by the ALA Council.

Intellectual Freedom Principles for Academic Libraries

An Interpretation of the Library Bill of Rights

A strong intellectual freedom perspective is critical to the development of academic library collections and services that dispassionately meet the education and research needs of a college or university community. The purpose of this statement is to outline how and where intellectual freedom principles fit into an academic library setting, thereby raising consciousness of the intellectual freedom context within which academic librarians work. The following principles should be reflected in all relevant library policy documents.

1. The general principles set forth in the *Library Bill of Rights* form an indispensable framework for building collections, services, and policies that serve the entire academic community.

2. The privacy of library users is and must be inviolable. Policies should be in place that maintain confidentiality of library borrowing records and of other information relating to personal use of library information and services.

3. The development of library collections in support of an institution's instruction and research programs should transcend the personal values of the selector. In the interests of research and learning, it is essential that collections contain materials representing a variety of perspectives on subjects that may be considered controversial.

4. Preservation and replacement efforts should ensure that balance in library materials is maintained and that controversial materials are not removed from the collections through theft, loss, mutilation, or normal wear and tear. There should be alertness to efforts by special interest groups to bias a collection though systematic theft or mutilation.

5. Licensing agreements should be consistent with the *Library Bill of Rights,* and should maximize access.

6. Open and unfiltered access to the Internet should be conveniently available to the academic community in

a college or university library. Content filtering devices and content-based restrictions are a contradiction of the academic library mission to further research and learning through exposure to the broadest possible range of ideas and information. Such restrictions are a fundamental violation of intellectual freedom in academic libraries.

7. Freedom of information and of creative expression should be reflected in library exhibits and in all relevant library policy documents.

8. Library meeting rooms, research carrels, exhibit spaces, and other facilities should be available to the academic community regardless of research being pursued or subject being discussed. Any restrictions made necessary because of limited availability of space should be based on need, as reflected in library policy, rather than on content of research or discussion.

9. Whenever possible, library services should be available without charge in order to encourage inquiry. Where charges are necessary, a free or low-cost alternative (e.g., downloading to disc rather than printing) should be available when possible.

10. A service philosophy should be promoted that affords equal access to information for all in the academic community with no discrimination on the basis of race, values, gender, sexual orientation, cultural or ethnic background, physical or learning disability, economic status, religious beliefs, or views.

11. A procedure ensuring due process should be in place to deal with requests by those within and outside the academic community for removal or addition of library resources, exhibits, or services.

12. It is recommended that this statement of principle be endorsed by appropriate institutional governing bodies, including the faculty senate or similar instrument of faculty governance.

Approved by ACRL Board of Directors June 29, 1999; adopted July 12, 2000, by the ALA Council.

Diversity in Collection Development

An Interpretation of the Library Bill of Rights

Collection development should reflect the philosophy inherent in Article II of the *Library Bill of Rights:* "Libraries should provide materials and information presenting all points of view on current and historical issues. Materials should not be proscribed or removed because of partisan or doctrinal disapproval." Library collections must represent the diversity of people and ideas in our society. There are many complex facets to any issue, and many contexts in which issues may be expressed, discussed, or interpreted. Librarians have an obligation to select and support access to materials and resources on all subjects that meet, as closely as possible, the needs, interests, and abilities of all persons in the community the library serves.

Librarians have a professional responsibility to be inclusive, not exclusive, in collection development and in the provision of interlibrary loan. Access to all materials and resources legally obtainable should be assured to the user, and policies should not unjustly exclude materials and resources even if they are offensive to the librarian or the user. This includes materials and resources that reflect a diversity of political, economic, religious, social, minority, and sexual issues. A balanced collection reflects a diversity of materials and resources, not an equality of numbers.

Collection development responsibilities include selecting materials and resources in different formats produced by independent, small and local producers as well as information resources from major producers and distributors. Materials and resources should represent the languages commonly used in the library's service community and should include formats that meet the needs of users with disabilities. Collection development and the selection of materials and resources should be done according to professional standards and established selection and review procedures. Librarians may seek to increase user awareness of materials and resources on various social concerns by many means, including, but not limited to, issuing lists of resources, arranging exhibits, and presenting programs.

Over time, individuals, groups, and entities have sought to limit the diversity of library collections. They cite a variety of reasons that include prejudicial language and ideas, political content, economic theory, social philosophies, religious beliefs, sexual content and expression, and other potentially controversial topics. Examples of such censorship may include removing or not selecting materials because they are considered by some as racist or sexist; not purchasing conservative religious materials; not selecting resources about or by minorities because it is thought these groups or interests are not represented in a community; or not providing information or materials from or about non-mainstream political entities. Librarians have a professional responsibility to be fair, just, and equitable and to give all library users equal protection in guarding against violation of the library patron's right to read, view, or listen to materials and resources protected by the First Amendment, no matter what the viewpoint of the author, creator, or selector. Librarians have an obligation to protect library collections from removal of materials and resources based on personal bias or prejudice.

Intellectual freedom, the essence of equitable library services, provides for free access to all expressions of ideas through which any and all sides of a question, cause, or movement may be explored. Toleration is meaningless without tolerance for what some may consider detestable. Librarians must not permit their own preferences to limit their degree of tolerance in collection development.

Adopted July 14, 1982, by the ALA Council; amended January 10, 1990; July 2, 2008.

Evaluating Library Collections

An Interpretation of the Library Bill of Rights

The continuous review of library materials is necessary as a means of maintaining an active library collection of current interest to users. In the process, materials may be added and physically deteriorated or obsolete materials may be replaced or removed in accordance with the collection maintenance policy of a given library and the needs of the community it serves. Continued evaluation is closely related to the goals and responsibilities of each library and is a valuable tool of collection development. This procedure is not to be used as a convenient means to remove materials that might be viewed as controversial or objectionable. Such abuse of the evaluation function violates the principles of intellectual freedom and is in opposition to the Preamble and Articles I and II of the *Library Bill of Rights,* which state:

> The American Library Association affirms that all libraries are forums for information and ideas, and that the following basic policies should guide their services.

I. Books and other library resources should be provided for the interest, information, and enlightenment of all people of the community the library serves. Materials should not be excluded because of the origin, background, or views of those contributing to their creation.

II. Libraries should provide materials and information presenting all points of view on current and historical issues. Materials should not be proscribed or removed because of partisan or doctrinal disapproval.

The American Library Association opposes internal censorship and strongly urges that libraries adopt guidelines setting forth the positive purposes and principles of evaluation of materials in library collections.

Adopted February 2, 1973, by the ALA Council; amended July 1, 1981; July 2, 2008.

Challenged Materials

An Interpretation of the Library Bill of Rights

The American Library Association declares as a matter of firm principle that it is the responsibility of every library to have a clearly defined materials selection policy in written form that reflects the *Library Bill of Rights,* and that is approved by the appropriate governing authority.

Challenged materials that meet the criteria for selection in the materials selection policy of the library should not be removed under any legal or extra-legal pressure. The *Library Bill of Rights* states in Article I that "Materials should not be excluded because of the origin, background, or views of those contributing to their creation," and in Article II, that "Materials should not be proscribed or removed because of partisan or doctrinal disap-proval." Freedom of expression is protected by the Constitution of the United States, but constitutionally protected expression is often separated from unprotected expression only by a dim and uncertain line. The Constitution requires a procedure designed to focus searchingly on challenged expression before it can be suppressed. An adversary hearing is a part of this procedure.

Therefore, any attempt, be it legal or extra-legal, to regulate or suppress materials in libraries must be closely scrutinized to the end that protected expression is not abridged.

Adopted June 25, 1971; amended July 1, 1981; amended January 10, 1990, by the ALA Council.

Expurgation of Library Materials

An Interpretation of the Library Bill of Rights

Expurgating library materials is a violation of the *Library Bill of Rights*. Expurgation as defined by this interpretation includes any deletion, excision, alteration, editing, or obliteration of any part(s) of books or other library resources by the library, its agents, or its parent institution (if any) when done for the purposes of censorship. Such action stands in violation of Articles I, II, and III of the *Library Bill of Rights,* which state that "Materials should not be excluded because of the origin, background, or views of those contributing to their creation," that "Materials should not be proscribed or removed because of partisan or doctrinal disapproval," and that "Libraries should challenge censorship in the fulfillment of their responsibility to provide information and enlightenment."

The act of expurgation denies access to the complete work and the entire spectrum of ideas that the work is intended to express. This is censorship. Expurgation based on the premise that certain portions of a work may be harmful to minors is equally a violation of the *Library Bill of Rights.*

Expurgation without permission from the rights holder may violate the copyright provisions of the United States Code.

The decision of rights holders to alter or expurgate future versions of a work does not impose a duty on librarians to alter or expurgate earlier versions of a work. Librarians should resist such requests in the interest of historical preservation and opposition to censorship. Furthermore, librarians oppose expurgation of resources available through licensed collections. Expurgation of any library resource imposes a restriction, without regard to the rights and desires of all library users, by limiting access to ideas and information.

Adopted February 2, 1973, by the ALA Council; amended July 1, 1981; January 10, 1990; July 2, 2008.

Restricted Access to Library Materials

An Interpretation of the Library Bill of Rights

Libraries are a traditional forum for the open exchange of information. Attempts to restrict access to library materials violate the basic tenets of the *Library Bill of Rights*.

Some libraries place materials in a "closed shelf," "locked case," "adults only," "restricted shelf," or "high-demand" collection. Some libraries have applied filtering software to their Internet stations to prevent users from finding targeted categories of information, much of which is constitutionally protected. Some libraries block access to certain materials by placing other barriers between the user and those materials.

Because restricted materials often deal with controversial, unusual, or sensitive subjects, having to ask a librarian or circulation clerk for access to them may be embarrassing or inhibiting for patrons desiring the materials. Requiring a user to ask for materials may create a service barrier or pose a language-skills barrier. Even when a title is listed in the catalog with a reference to its restricted status, a barrier is placed between the patron and the publication. (See also "Labels and Rating Systems.") Because restricted materials often feature information that some people consider objectionable, potential library users may be predisposed to think of the materials as objectionable and, therefore, be reluctant to ask for access to them.

Limiting access by relegating materials into physically or virtually restricted or segregated collections or restricting materials by creating age-related, linguistic, economic, psychological, or other barriers violates the *Library Bill of Rights*. However, some libraries have established restrictive policies to protect their materials from theft or mutilation, or because of statutory authority or institutional mandate. Such policies must be carefully formulated and administered to ensure they do not violate established principles of intellectual freedom. This caution is reflected in ALA policies, such as "Evaluating Library Collections," "Free Access to Libraries for Minors," "Preservation Policy," and the ACRL "Code of Ethics for Special Collections Librarians."

In keeping with the "Joint Statement on Access" of the American Library Association and Society of American Archivists, libraries should avoid accepting donor agreements or entering into contracts that impose permanent restrictions on special collections. As stated in the "Joint Statement," it is the responsibility of libraries with such collections "to make available original research materials in its possession on equal terms of access."

All proposals for restricted access collections should be carefully scrutinized to ensure that the purpose is not to suppress a viewpoint or to place a barrier between certain patrons and particular content. A primary goal of the library profession is to facilitate access to all points of view on current and historical issues.

Adopted February 2, 1973; amended July 1, 1981; July 3, 1991; July 12, 2000; June 30, 2004, by the ALA Council.

Access to Electronic Information, Services, and Networks

An Interpretation of the Library Bill of Rights

INTRODUCTION

Freedom of expression is an inalienable human right and the foundation for self-government. Freedom of expression encompasses the freedom of speech and the corollary right to receive information.[1] Libraries and librarians protect and promote these rights by selecting, producing, providing access to, identifying, retrieving, organizing, providing instruction in the use of, and preserving recorded expression regardless of the format or technology.

The American Library Association expresses these basic principles of librarianship in its *Code of Ethics* and in the *Library Bill of Rights* and its Interpretations. These serve to guide librarians and library governing bodies in addressing issues of intellectual freedom that arise when the library provides access to electronic information, services, and networks.

Libraries empower users by providing access to the broadest range of information. Electronic resources, including information available via the Internet, allow libraries to fulfill this responsibility better than ever before.

Issues arising from digital generation, distribution, and retrieval of information need to be approached and regularly reviewed from a context of constitutional principles and ALA policies so that fundamental and traditional tenets of librarianship are not swept away.

Electronic information flows across boundaries and barriers despite attempts by individuals, governments, and private entities to channel or control it. Even so, many people lack access or capability to use electronic information effectively.

In making decisions about how to offer access to electronic information, each library should consider its mission, goals, objectives, cooperative agreements, and the needs of the entire community it serves.

THE RIGHTS OF USERS

All library system and network policies, procedures, or regulations relating to electronic information and services should be scrutinized for potential violation of user rights.

User policies should be developed according to the policies and guidelines established by the American Library Association, including *Guidelines for the Development and Implementation of Policies, Regulations and Procedures Affecting Access to Library Materials, Services and Facilities.*

Users' access should not be restricted or denied for expressing or receiving constitutionally protected speech. If access is restricted or denied for behavioral or other reasons, users should be provided due process, including, but not limited to, formal notice and a means of appeal.

Information retrieved or utilized electronically is constitutionally protected unless determined otherwise by a court of law with appropriate jurisdiction. These rights extend to minors as well as adults (*Free Access to Libraries for Minors; Access to Resources and Services in the School Library Media Program; Access for Children and Young People to Videotapes and Other Nonprint Formats*).[2]

Libraries should use technology to enhance, not deny, access to information. Users have the right to be free of unreasonable limitations or conditions set by libraries, librarians, system administrators, vendors, network service providers, or others.

Contracts, agreements, and licenses entered into by libraries on behalf of their users should not violate this right. Libraries should provide library users the training and assistance necessary to find, evaluate, and use information effectively.

Users have both the right of confidentiality and the right of privacy. The library should uphold these rights by policy, procedure, and practice in accordance with *Privacy: An Interpretation of the Library Bill of Rights.*

EQUITY OF ACCESS

The Internet provides expanding opportunities for everyone to participate in the information society, but too many individuals face serious barriers to access. Libraries play a critical role in bridging information access gaps for these individuals. Libraries also ensure that the public can find content of interest and learn the necessary skills to use information successfully.

Electronic information, services, and networks provided directly or indirectly by the library should be equally, readily and equitably accessible to all library users. American Library Association policies oppose the charging of user fees for the provision of information services by libraries that receive their major support from public funds (50.3 *Free Access to Information;* 53.1.14 *Economic Barriers to Information Access;* 60.1.1 Minority Concerns Policy Objectives; 61.1 Library Services for the Poor Policy Objectives). All libraries should develop policies concerning access to electronic information that are consistent with ALA's policy statements, including *Economic Barriers to Information Access: An Interpretation of the Library Bill of Rights, Guidelines for the Development and Implementation of Policies, Regulations and Procedures Affecting Access to Library Materials, Services and Facilities,* and *Resolution on Access to the Use of Libraries and Information by Individuals with Physical or Mental Impairment.*

INFORMATION RESOURCES AND ACCESS

Providing connections to global information, services, and networks is not the same as selecting and purchasing materials for a library collection. Determining the accuracy or authenticity of electronic information may present special problems. Some information accessed electronically may not meet a library's selection or collection development policy. It is, therefore, left to each user to determine what is appropriate. Parents and legal guardians who are concerned about their children's use of electronic resources should provide guidance to their own children.

Libraries, acting within their mission and objectives, must support access to information on all subjects that serve the needs or interests of each user, regardless of the user's age or the content of the material. In order to preserve the cultural record and to prevent the loss of information, libraries may need to expand their selection or collection development policies to ensure preservation, in appropriate formats, of information obtained electronically. Libraries have an obligation to provide access to government information available in electronic format.

Libraries and librarians should not deny or limit access to electronic information because of its allegedly controversial content or because of the librarian's personal beliefs or fear of confrontation. Furthermore, libraries and librarians should not deny access to electronic information solely on the grounds that it is perceived to lack value.

Publicly funded libraries have a legal obligation to provide access to constitutionally protected information. Federal, state, county, municipal, local, or library governing bodies sometimes require the use of Internet filters or other technological measures that block access to constitutionally protected information, contrary to the *Library Bill of Rights* (ALA *Policy Manual*, 53.1.17, *Resolution on the Use of Filtering Software in Libraries*). If a library uses a technological measure that blocks access to information, it should be set at the least restrictive level in order to minimize the blocking of constitutionally protected speech. Adults retain the right to access all constitutionally protected information and to ask for the technological measure to be disabled in a timely manner. Minors also retain the right to access constitutionally protected information and, at the minimum, have the right to ask the library or librarian to provide access to erroneously blocked information in a timely manner. Libraries and librarians have an obligation to inform users of these rights and to provide the means to exercise these rights.[3]

Electronic resources provide unprecedented opportunities to expand the scope of information available to users. Libraries and librarians should provide access to information presenting all points of view. The provision of access does not imply sponsorship or endorsement. These principles pertain to electronic resources no less than they do to the more traditional sources of information in libraries (*Diversity in Collection Development*).

NOTES

1. *Martin v. Struthers,* 319 U.S. 141 (1943); *Lamont v. Postmaster General,* 381 U.S. 301 (1965); Susan Nevelow Mart, "The Right to Receive Information," 95 *Law Library Journal* 2 (2003).

2. *Tinker v. Des Moines Independent Community School District,* 393 U.S. 503 (1969); *Board of Education, Island Trees Union Free School District No. 26 v. Pico,* 457 U.S. 853 (1982); *American Amusement Machine Association v. Teri Kendrick,* 244 F.3d 954 (7th Cir. 2001); cert. denied, 534 U.S. 994 (2001)

3. "If some libraries do not have the capacity to unblock specific Web sites or to disable the filter or if it is shown that an adult user's election to view constitutionally protected Internet material is burdened in some other substantial way, that would be the subject for an as-applied challenge, not the facial challenge made in this case." *United States, et al. v. American Library Association,* 539 U.S. 194 (2003) (Justice Kennedy, concurring).

See also "Questions and Answers on Access to Electronic Information, Services and Networks: An Interpretation of the Library Bill of Rights."

Adopted January 24, 1996; amended January 19, 2005, by the ALA Council.

Guidelines and Considerations for Developing a Public Library Internet Use Policy

INTELLECTUAL FREEDOM'S MEANING AND SCOPE

Libraries are a major information source in our society for access to the larger world of human expression. For some, they are the only available access point. Libraries connect individuals with the ideas, information, and images they seek. Libraries that raise barriers to access damage their credibility with their users.

By providing information across the spectrum of human interests, and making them available and accessible to anyone who wants them, libraries allow individuals to exercise their First Amendment right to seek and receive all types of expression, from all points of view. Materials in any given library cover the spectrum of human experience and thought, even those that some people may consider false, offensive, or dangerous.

In the millions of Web sites available on the Internet, there are some—often loosely called "pornography"—that parents, or adults generally, do not want children to see. A very small fraction of those sexually explicit materials is actual obscenity or child pornography, which are not constitutionally protected. The rest, like the overwhelming majority of materials on the Internet, is protected by the First Amendment.

Obscenity and child pornography are illegal. Federal and state statutes, the latter varying slightly depending on the jurisdiction, proscribe such materials. The U.S. Supreme Court has settled most questions about what obscenity and child pornography statutes are constitutionally sound.

According to the Court:

Obscenity must be determined using a three-part test. To be obscene, (1) the average person, applying contemporary community standards, must find that the work, taken as a whole, appeals to prurient interests; (2) the work must depict or describe, in a patently offensive way, sexual conduct as specified in the applicable statutes; and (3) the work, taken as a whole, must lack serious literary, artistic, political, or scientific value.

Child pornography may be determined using a slightly less rigorous test. To be child pornography, the work must involve depictions of sexual conduct specified in the applicable statutes and use images of children below a specified age.

Many states and some localities have "harmful to minors" laws. These laws regulate free speech with respect to minors, typically forbidding the display or dissemination of certain sexually explicit materials to children, as further specified in the laws.

According to the U.S. Supreme Court:

Materials "harmful to minors" include descriptions or representations of nudity, sexual conduct, or sexual excitement that appeal to the prurient, shameful, or morbid interest of minors; are patently offensive to prevailing standards in the adult community as a whole with respect to what is suitable material for minors; and lack serious literary, artistic, political, or scientific value for minors.

Knowing what materials are actually obscenity or child pornography is difficult, as is knowing, when minors are involved, and what materials are actually "harmful to minors." The applicable statutes and laws, together with the written decisions of courts that have applied them in actual cases, are the only official guides. Libraries and librarians are *not* in a position to make those decisions for library users or for citizens generally. Only courts have constitutional authority to determine, in accordance with due process, what materials are obscenity, child pornography, or "harmful to minors."

Obscenity and child pornography statutes apply to materials on the Internet; such materials are currently being regulated there. The applicability of particular "harmful to minors" laws to materials on the Internet is unsettled, however. Because of the uncertainty, various federal and state legislative proposals are pending specifically to "protect" children from sexually explicit materials on the Internet.

INTELLECTUAL FREEDOM'S FIRST AMENDMENT FOUNDATIONS

Courts have held that the public library is a "limited public forum." "Limited" means it is a place for access to free and open communication, subject to reasonable restrictions as to the time, place, and manner for doing so. As with any public forum the government has opened for people to use for communication, the First Amendment protects people's right to use the forum without the government interfering with what is communicated there. This is the very essence of the Constitution's guarantee of freedom of speech.

In a public forum, the government is prohibited from exercising discrimination with respect to the *content* of communication, unless the government demonstrates that the restriction is necessary to achieve a "compelling" government interest and there is no less restrictive alternative for achieving that interest. This means public libraries cannot exclude books about abortion just because they discuss the subject of abortion. That would be discrimination with respect to *content*. Books can be selected on the basis of content-neutral criteria such as the quality of the writing, their position on best-seller lists, the presence or absence of other materials in the collection related to certain time periods or historical figures, and the like; they can be deselected on the basis of wear and tear, the availability of more current materials, and similar criteria. Libraries, however, cannot deliberately suppress the record of human thought on a particular subject or topic.

Internet filters are mechanisms designed to discriminate with respect to the *content* of communication. Filters are incapable of doing what computer software engineers have designed them to do—typically, to block only "hard-core pornography" and other "offensive" sites on the Internet. But even at their hypothetical best, mechanisms to screen and block content on the Internet exclude far more than just obscenity and child pornography. They exclude a wide range of sexually explicit materials protected under the Constitution. For instance, materials that depict homosexual relations, variations on conventional heterosexuality, and even nudity and heterosexual relations channeled toward reproduction and family life represent distinct subjects or topics. Their suppression is discrimination with respect to the *content* of communication.

The rapid expansion of Web sites on the Internet and the sheer impossibility of keeping up with this growth are factors that limit the reliability of filtering devices. Neither humans nor machines are capable of processing and reviewing everything available, with the result that filters will block some materials while other equivalent materials will remain unblocked.

Moreover, there is legal precedent that suggests that government agencies like libraries cannot adopt and enforce private rating schemes. When libraries restrict access based on content ratings developed and applied by a filtering vendor, sometimes with no knowledge of how these ratings are applied or what sites have been restricted, they are delegating their public responsibility to a private agency.

Filtering and other means to block content on the Internet can be utilized only if the government—in this case, the public library—can demonstrate both that the need is compelling and that the method chosen to achieve the purpose is the least restrictive method possible. The lawsuit brought by the American Library Association—*American Library Ass'n v. United States Department of Justice,* consolidated with and decided by the U.S. Supreme Court under the name of *Reno v. American Civil Liberties Union*—invalidated the provisions of the Communications Decency Act of 1996 that criminalized "indecent" and "patently offensive" electronic communication. The Court did so on the ground that those provisions, suppressing speech addressed to adults, reduced the entire population only to what is fit for children. It recognized "the governmental interest in protecting children from harmful materials," but found that less restrictive means were available to achieve that interest.

It is well documented that filtering software is over-inclusive, blocking not only sites that may have sexual content, strong language, or unconventional ideas considered harmful or offensive—but also sites having no controversial content whatsoever. This over-inclusive blocking violates the First Amendment rights of youth and children, as well as adults, to access constitutionally protected materials. In the context of limiting or avoiding children's exposure to possibly "harmful" materials on library computers with Internet access, less restrictive means than the use of filters are available.

Adults' reading cannot be reduced to the level of what is fit for children, and the public library, therefore, cannot restrict them to Internet-access computers with filtering software. Young adults and children also have First Amendment rights, although such rights are variable, depending on the age of the minor and other factors, including maturity, not yet settled in the law. Even though minors' First Amendment rights are not as extensive as those of adults, the public library cannot restrict them solely to computers with filtering software. This is why libraries advocate that parents guide their children's use of the Internet. Only unfiltered Internet access accommodates both parental guidance and sensitive recognition of the First Amendment rights of young people.

Librarians and the strength of their commitment to professional standards and values assure that, at least through the public library, the least restrictive means available to achieve the government's interest in protecting children will be implemented.

SPECIFIC INTERNET USE POLICY PROVISIONS

The position of the American Library Association is set forth in several documents adopted by the Council, its governing body. The *Interpretation of the Library Bill of Rights* entitled *Access to Electronic Information, Services, and Networks* calls for free and unfettered access to the Internet for any library user, regardless of age. The *Resolution on the Use of Filtering Software in Libraries* and the *Statement on Library Use of Filtering Software* reiterate the U.S. Supreme Court's declaration in *Reno v. American Civil Liberties Union* that the Internet is a forum of free expression deserving full constitutional protection. The *Resolution* and *Statement* condemn as a violation of the *Library Bill of Rights* any use of filtering software by libraries that blocks access to constitutionally protected speech.

Consistent with these policies, which collectively embody the library profession's understanding of First Amendment constraints on library Internet use, the Intellectual Freedom Committee offers guidelines to public libraries, as follows:

Adopt a comprehensive, written Internet use policy that, among other things should

- set forth reasonable time, place, and manner restrictions;
- expressly prohibit any use of library equipment to access material that is obscene, child pornography, or "harmful to minors" (consistent with any applicable state or local law);
- provide for the privacy of users with respect to public terminals; and
- protect the confidentiality of records, electronic or otherwise, that identify individual users and link them to search strategies, sites accessed, or other specific data about the information they retrieved or sought to retrieve.

Communicate the relevant policies for use of Internet-access computers to all library users, and include the parents of children who may use the library without direct parental supervision. Do so in a clear and conspicuous manner sufficient to alert library users that filtering software is not utilized.

Post notices at all Internet-access computers that use of library equipment to access the illegal materials specified in the Internet use policy is prohibited.

Offer a variety of programs, at convenient times, to educate library users, including parents and children, on the use of the Internet. Publicize them widely.

Offer library users recommended Internet sites. For youth and children, especially, offer them, according to age group, direct links to sites with educational and other types of material best suited to their typical needs and interests (e.g., the American Library Association's *700+ Great Sites for Kids and the Adults Who Care about Them* and its Internet guide for young adults, *TEENHoopla*).

Samples of Internet Use Polices are located on the Office for Intellectual Freedom's Web page, "Internet Use Policies," at [www.ala.org/ala/aboutala/offices/oif/ifissues/issuesrelatedlinks/internetusepolicies.cfm].

ANSWERS TO OBJECTIONS

Various metaphors have been offered, both by opponents of free and open access in libraries, as well as proponents, to explain the use of the Internet in libraries and the impact of filtering software. Two metaphors offered by opponents and the arguments built around them deserve close examination:

The "selection" metaphor. Filtering Internet resources is tantamount to selecting materials in a library. Since libraries, opponents of unfettered Internet access say, are not constrained to select any particular materials for their collections, filtering is constitutionally unobjectionable.

This metaphor is faulty. Filtering the Internet is not selecting materials. The only selection decisions involved in use of the Internet in libraries are those as to whether, for instance, the World Wide Web will be offered with other tools based on special Internet protocols, e.g., *ftp* (file transfer protocol) or *telnet*. Selecting the World Wide Web for the library means selecting the entire resource, just as selecting *Time* means selecting the entire magazine. A library cannot select *Time* and then decide to redact or rip out the pages constituting the "American Scene" feature or the "Washington Diary." That would be censorship. It is the same with the World Wide Web. It is not an accident of terminology that the Web consists of a vast number of Web *pages* and that browser software permits the user to *bookmark* those that are interesting or useful.

The "interlibrary loan" metaphor. Internet access is tantamount to interlibrary loan service. Typing a Web site URL into a browser's location entry box and pressing the Enter key amounts to an interlibrary loan request that the library, opponents of unfettered access say, is free to deny.

This metaphor is faulty, too. Far more frequently than typing and entering URLs, surfers of the World Wide Web click on hot links for automatic access to the Web pages they wish to see. More significantly, absent financial constraints, any public library true to its function as a public forum makes available to users any constitutionally protected material, whether that means locating the material within the library itself or obtaining it elsewhere through interlibrary loan.

As articulated by the U.S. Supreme Court in the American Library Association case culminating in *Reno v. American Civil Liberties Union,* the Internet represents a vast library. It is a virtual library already present within any public library that selects Internet access. The fundamental First Amendment question is: given the free availability of a near-infinite range of content on the Internet, can the library ever deliberately deprive a library user of the constitutionally protected materials he or she seeks? The emphatic answer of the librarian informed by principles of intellectual freedom is: *absolutely not.*

But what about obscenity and child pornography, as well as, when minors are involved, materials "harmful to minors"?

- As for obscenity and child pornography, prosecutors and police have adequate tools to enforce criminal laws. Libraries are not a component of law enforcement efforts naturally directed toward the source, i.e., the publishers, of such material.

- As for materials "harmful to minors," it is true that, in *some* jurisdictions, libraries that choose not to utilize filtering or other means to block content on the Internet may find themselves in a "bind"; under some circumstances, they may be subject to liability under "harmful to minors" laws.

Libraries should be cautioned that laws differ from state to state, and they should seek advice on laws applicable in their jurisdiction from counsel versed in First Amendment principles. In particular, they should determine whether any "harmful to minors" law applies to materials available at the library, either through Internet access or otherwise. They should specifically inquire whether they are expressly exempt from the particular "harmful to minors" laws in their jurisdiction, as libraries frequently are.

Moreover, libraries should be aware that the legal framework and context of regulation is rapidly changing; federal, state, and local governments have begun to legislate specifically in the area of library Internet use. Libraries should actively oppose proposed legislation that exposes them to new liabilities and negatively impacts intellectual freedom. As always, they should be vigilant about new regulations of free speech.

For information on filtering and other legal issues affecting libraries, see the Freedom to Read Foundation's Web page, "Memoranda to Freedom to Read Foundation from Jenner & Block" (its legal counsel) at [www.ala.org/ala/mgrps/othergroups/freedomtoreadfoundation/ftrfinaction/jennerblockmemo/jennerblockmemoranda.cfm], and the Office for Intellectual Freedom's Web page, "Filters and Filtering," at [www.ala.org/ala/aboutala/offices/oif/ifissues/filtersfiltering.cfm].

Issued June 1998; rev. November 2000.

Exhibit Spaces and Bulletin Boards

An Interpretation of the Library Bill of Rights

Libraries often provide exhibit spaces and bulletin boards. The uses made of these spaces should conform to the *Library Bill of Rights:* Article I states, "Materials should not be excluded because of the origin, background, or views of those contributing to their creation." Article II states, "Materials should not be proscribed or removed because of partisan or doctrinal disapproval." Article VI maintains that exhibit space should be made available "on an equitable basis, regardless of the beliefs or affiliations of individuals or groups requesting their use."

In developing library exhibits, staff members should endeavor to present a broad spectrum of opinion and a variety of viewpoints. Libraries should not shrink from developing exhibits because of controversial content or because of the beliefs or affiliations of those whose work is represented. Just as libraries do not endorse the viewpoints of those whose work is represented in their collections, libraries also do not endorse the beliefs or viewpoints of topics that may be the subject of library exhibits.

Exhibit areas often are made available for use by community groups. Libraries should formulate a written policy for the use of these exhibit areas to assure that space is provided on an equitable basis to all groups that request it.

Written policies for exhibit space use should be stated in inclusive rather than exclusive terms. For example, a policy that the library's exhibit space is open "to organizations engaged in educational, cultural, intellectual, or charitable activities" is an inclusive statement of the limited uses of the exhibit space. This defined limitation would permit religious groups to use the exhibit space because they engage in intellectual activities, but would exclude most commercial uses of the exhibit space.

A publicly supported library may designate use of exhibit space for strictly library-related activities, provided that this limitation is viewpoint neutral and clearly defined.

Libraries may include in this policy rules regarding the time, place, and manner of use of the exhibit space, so long as the rules are content neutral and are applied in the same manner to all groups wishing to use the space. A library may wish to limit access to exhibit space to groups within the community served by the library. This practice is acceptable provided that the same rules and regulations apply to everyone, and that exclusion is not made on the basis of the doctrinal, religious, or political beliefs of the potential users.

The library should not censor or remove an exhibit because some members of the community may disagree with its content. Those who object to the content of any exhibit held at the library should be able to submit their complaint and/or their own exhibit proposal to be judged according to the policies established by the library.

Libraries may wish to post a permanent notice near the exhibit area stating that the library does not advocate or endorse the viewpoints of exhibits or exhibitors.

Libraries that make bulletin boards available to public groups for posting notices of public interest should develop criteria for the use of these spaces based on the same considerations as those outlined above. Libraries may wish to develop criteria regarding the size of material to be displayed, the length of time materials may remain on the bulletin board, the frequency with which material may be posted for the same group, and the geographic area from which notices will be accepted.

Adopted July 2, 1991, by the ALA Council; amended June 30, 2004, by the ALA Council.

Library-Initiated Programs as a Resource

An Interpretation of the Library Bill of Rights

Library-initiated programs support the mission of the library by providing users with additional opportunities for information, education, and recreation. Article I of the *Library Bill of Rights* states: "Books and other library resources should be provided for the interest, information, and enlightenment of all people of the community the library serves."

Library-initiated programs take advantage of library staff expertise, collections, services and facilities to increase access to information and information resources. Library-initiated programs introduce users and potential users to the resources of the library and to the library's primary function as a facilitator of information access. The library may participate in cooperative or joint programs with other agencies, organizations, institutions, or individuals as part of its own effort to address information needs and to facilitate information access in the community the library serves.

Library-initiated programs on site and in other locations include, but are not limited to, speeches, community forums, discussion groups, demonstrations, displays, and live or media presentations.

Libraries serving multilingual or multicultural communities should make efforts to accommodate the information needs of those for whom English is a second language. Library-initiated programs that cross language and cultural barriers introduce otherwise underserved populations to the resources of the library and provide access to information.

Library-initiated programs "should not be proscribed or removed [or canceled] because of partisan or doctrinal disapproval" of the contents of the program or the views expressed by the participants, as stated in Article II of the *Library Bill of Rights*. Library sponsorship of a program does not constitute an endorsement of the content of the program or the views expressed by the participants, any more than the purchase of material for the library collection constitutes an endorsement of the contents of the material or the views of its creator.

Library-initiated programs are a library resource, and, as such, are developed in accordance with written guidelines, as approved and adopted by the library's policy-making body. These guidelines should include an endorsement of the *Library*

Bill of Rights and set forth the library's commitment to free and open access to information and ideas for all users.

Library staff select topics, speakers and resource materials for library-initiated programs based on the interests and information needs of the community. Topics, speakers and resource materials are not excluded from library-initiated programs because of possible controversy. Concerns, questions or complaints about library-initiated programs are handled according to the same written policy and procedures that govern reconsiderations of other library resources.

Library-initiated programs are offered free of charge and are open to all. Article V of the *Library Bill of Rights* states:

"A person's right to use a library should not be denied or abridged because of origin, age, background, or views."

The "right to use a library" encompasses all the resources the library offers, including the right to attend library-initiated programs. Libraries do not deny or abridge access to library resources, including library-initiated programs, based on an individual's economic background or ability to pay.

Adopted January 27, 1982; amended June 26, 1990; July 12, 2000, by the ALA Council.

Meeting Rooms

An Interpretation of the Library Bill of Rights

Many libraries provide meeting rooms for individuals and groups as part of a program of service. Article VI of the *Library Bill of Rights* states that such facilities should be made available to the public served by the given library "on an equitable basis, regardless of the beliefs or affiliations of individuals or groups requesting their use."

Libraries maintaining meeting room facilities should develop and publish policy statements governing use. These statements can properly define time, place, or manner of use; such qualifications should not pertain to the content of a meeting or to the beliefs or affiliations of the sponsors. These statements should be made available in any commonly used language within the community served.

If meeting rooms in libraries supported by public funds are made available to the general public for non-library sponsored events, the library may not exclude any group based on the subject matter to be discussed or based on the ideas that the group advocates. For example, if a library allows charities and sports clubs to discuss their activities in library meeting rooms, then the library should not exclude partisan political or religious groups from discussing their actives in the same facilities. If a library opens its meeting rooms to a wide variety of civic organizations, then the library may not deny access to a religious organization. Libraries may wish to post a permanent notice near the meeting room stating that the library does not advocate or endorse the viewpoints of meeting or meeting room users.

Written policies for meeting room use should be stated in inclusive rather than exclusive terms. For example, a policy that the library's facilities are open "to organizations engaged in educational, cultural, intellectual or charitable activities" is an inclusive statement of the limited uses to which the facilities may be put. This defined limitation would permit religious groups to use the facilities because they engage in intellectual activities, but would exclude most commercial uses of the facility.

A publicly supported library may limit use of its meeting rooms to strictly "library-related" activities, provided that the limitation is clearly circumscribed and is viewpoint neutral.

Written policies may include limitations on frequency of use, and whether or not meetings held in library meeting rooms must be open to the public. If state and local laws permit private as well as public sessions of meetings in library, libraries may choose to offer both options. The same standard should be applicable to all.

If meetings are open to the public, libraries should include in their meeting room policy statement a section that addresses admission fees. If admission fees are permitted, libraries shall seek to make it possible that these fees do not limit access to individuals who may be unable to pay, but who wish to attend the meeting. Article V of the *Library Bill of Rights* states that "a person's right to use a library should not be denied or abridged because of origin, age, background, or views." It is inconsistent with Article V to restrict indirectly access to library meeting rooms based on an individual's or group's ability to pay for that access.

Adopted July 2, 1991, by the ALA Council.

Policy on Confidentiality of Library Records

The Council of the American Library Association strongly recommends that the responsible officers of each library, cooperative system, and consortium in the United States

1. Formally adopt a policy that specifically recognizes its circulation records and other records identifying the names of library users to be confidential. (See also *ALA Code of Ethics,* Article III, "We protect each library user's right to privacy and confidentiality with respect to information sought or received, and resources consulted, borrowed, acquired or transmitted" and *Privacy: An Interpretation of the Library Bill of Rights.*)

2. Advise all librarians and library employees that such records shall not be made available to any agency of state, federal, or local government except pursuant to such process, order or subpoena as may be authorized under the authority of, and pursuant to, federal, state, or local law relating to civil, criminal, or administrative discovery procedures or legislative investigative power.

3. Resist the issuance of enforcement of any such process, order, or subpoena until such time as a proper showing of good cause has been made in a court of competent jurisdiction.[1]

NOTE

1. Point 3, above, means that upon receipt of such process, order, or subpoena, the library's officers will consult with their legal counsel to determine if such process, order, or subpoena is in proper form and if there is a showing of good cause for its issuance; if the process, order, or subpoena is not in proper form or if good cause has not been shown, they will insist that such defects be cured.

Adopted January 20, 1971; revised July 4, 1975; July 2, 1986, by the ALA Council.

Suggested Procedures for Implementing "Policy on Confidentiality of Library Records"

When drafting local policies, libraries should consult with their legal counsel to ensure these policies are based upon and consistent with applicable federal, state, and local law concerning the confidentiality of library records, the disclosure of public records, and the protection of individual privacy. (See Interpretations to the *Library Bill of Rights,* including *Access to Electronic Information, Services, and Networks* and *Privacy.*)

Suggested procedures include the following:[1]

1. The library staff member receiving the request to examine or obtain information relating to circulation or other records identifying the names of library users must immediately refer the person making the request to the responsible officer of the institution, who shall explain the confidentiality policy.

2. The director, upon receipt of such process, order, or subpoena, shall consult with the appropriate legal officer assigned to the institution to determine if such process, order, or subpoena is in good form and if there is a showing of good cause for its issuance.

3. If the process, order, or subpoena is not in proper form or if good cause has not been shown, the library should insist that such defects be cured before any records are released.

4. The legal process requiring the production of circulation or other library records is ordinarily in the form of a subpoena *duces tecum* (bring your records) requiring the responsible library officer to attend court or to provide testimony at his or her deposition. It also may require him or her to bring along certain designated circulation or other specified records.

5. Staff should be trained and required to report any threats or unauthorized demands (e.g., those not supported by a process, order, or subpoena) concerning circulation and other records to the appropriate officer of the institution.

6. Any problems relating to the privacy of circulation and other records identifying the names of library users that are not provided for above shall be referred to the responsible officer.

NOTE

1. See also "Confidentiality and Coping with Law Enforcement Inquiries: Guidelines for the Library and Its Staff."

Adopted by the ALA Intellectual Freedom Committee, January 9, 1983; revised January 11, 1988; revised March 18, 2005.

Confidentiality and Coping with Law Enforcement Inquiries

Guidelines for the Library and Its Staff

Increased visits to libraries by law enforcement agents, including FBI agents and officers of state, county, and municipal police departments, are raising considerable concern among the public and the library community. These visits are not only a result of the increased surveillance and investigation prompted by the events of September 11, 2001, and the subsequent passage of the USA PATRIOT Act, but also as a result of law enforcement officers investigating computer crimes, including e-mail threats and possible violations of the laws addressing online obscenity and child pornography.

These guidelines, developed to assist libraries and library staff in dealing with law enforcement inquiries, rely upon the ALA's

- Privacy: An Interpretation of the Library Bill of Rights;

- Questions and Answers on Privacy and Confidentiality;

- Policy on Confidentiality of Library Records;

- Suggested Procedures for Implementing Policy on Confidentiality of Library Records;

- Policy concerning Confidentiality of Personally Identifiable Information about Library Users;

- Code of Ethics.

FUNDAMENTAL PRINCIPLES

Librarians' professional ethics require that personally identifiable information about library users be kept confidential. This principle is reflected in Article III of the Code of Ethics, which states that "[librarians] protect each library user's right to privacy and confidentiality with respect to information sought or received, and resources consulted, borrowed, acquired, or transmitted." Privacy: An Interpretation of the Library Bill of Rights, notes that "[p]rotecting user privacy and confidentiality has long been an integral part of the mission of libraries."

Currently, 48 states and the District of Columbia have laws protecting the confidentiality of library records, and the Attorneys General of the remaining two states, Hawaii and Kentucky, have ruled that library records are confidential and may not be disclosed under the laws governing open records. Confidential library records should not be released or made available in any format to a federal agent, law enforcement officer, or other person unless a court order in proper form has been entered by a court of competent jurisdiction after a showing of good cause by the law enforcement agency or person seeking the records.

GENERAL GUIDELINES

Confidentiality of library records is a basic principle of librarianship. As a matter of policy or procedure, the library administrator should ensure that

- The library staff and governing board are familiar with the ALA Policy on Confidentiality of Library Records, the Policy concerning Confidentiality of Personally Identifiable Information about Library Users, and other ALA documents on users' privacy and confidentiality.

- The library staff and governing board are familiar with their state's library confidentiality statute or attorney general's opinion.

- The library adopts a policy on users' privacy and confidentiality. Such policies should inform users about

their expectation of privacy and how the library handles their confidential information.

- The library adopts staff policies that inform the staff and board about the procedures to follow if the library is served with judicial process (search warrants or subpoenas) seeking library records or if law enforcement agents conduct inquiries in the library.

- The library staff is familiar with the library's policy on confidentiality and its procedures for handling court orders and law enforcement inquiries.

LIBRARY PROCEDURES AFFECT CONFIDENTIALITY

Law enforcement visits aside, be aware that library operating procedures have an impact on confidentiality. The following recommendations are suggestions to bring library procedures into compliance with most state confidentiality statutes, ALA policies on confidentiality and its *Code of Ethics:*

- Avoid creating unnecessary records. Only record a user's personally identifiable information when necessary for the efficient operation of the library.

- Avoid retaining records that are not needed for efficient operation of the library. Check with your local governing body to learn if there are laws or policies addressing record retention and in conformity with these laws or policies, develop policies on the length of time necessary to retain a record. Ensure that all kinds and types of records are covered by the policy, including data-related logs, digital records, and system backups.

- Once record retention policies are in place, ensure that records are destroyed or archived on schedule. A library cannot destroy records after it receives notice from law enforcement agents that the records may be subject to judicial process.

- Be aware of library practices and procedures that place information on public view. Some examples are the use of postcards for overdue notices or requested materials; staff terminals placed so that the screens can be read by the public; sign-in sheets to use computers or other devices; and the provision of titles of reserve requests or interlibrary loans provided over the telephone to users' family members or answering machines.

- Remember that there is no affirmative duty to collect or retain information about library patrons on behalf of law enforcement.

RECOMMENDED PROCEDURES FOR LAW ENFORCEMENT VISITS

Before any visit:

- Designate the person or persons who will be responsible for handling law enforcement requests. In most circumstances, it should be the library director, and, if available, the library's legal counsel.

- Review the library's confidentiality policy and state confidentiality law with library counsel. Communicate those policies and the requirements of the law to both staff and volunteer workers in the library.

- Train all library staff, *including volunteers,* on the library's procedure for handling law enforcement requests. They should understand that it is lawful to refer the agent or officer to an administrator in charge of the library, and that they do not need to respond immediately to any request.

- A court order may require the removal of a computer workstation or other computer storage device from the library. Have plans in place to address service interruptions and any necessary backups for equipment and software.

During the visit:

- Staff should immediately ask for identification if they are approached by an agent or law enforcement officer, and then record the information. If possible, verify the information with the local FBI office or the police department. The agent or officer should then be immediately referred to the library director or the designated supervisor.

- The director or supervisor should meet with the agent with another colleague in attendance. If possible, one person should take notes if a record of the encounter is needed in the future.

- If the agent or officer does not have a court order compelling the production of records, the library director should explain the library's confidentiality policy and the state's confidentiality law, and inform the agent or officer that users' records are not available except when a proper court order in good form has been presented to the library.

- Without a court order, neither the FBI nor local law enforcement has authority to compel cooperation with an investigation or require answers to questions, other than the name and address of the person speaking to the agent or officer. If the agent or officer persists, or makes an appeal to patriotism, the library director should explain that, as good citizens, the library staff will not respond to informal requests for confidential information, in conformity with professional ethics, First Amendment freedoms, and state law.

- If the agent or officer presents a search warrant or other judicial process, the library director should immediately call the library's counsel and ask for assistance.

If the judicial process is in the form of a subpoena:

- Remember that a subpoena does not require an immediate response from the library. Thank the officer serving the subpoena and inform him or her that the library will respond to the subpoena within the time allotted and in conformity with the law. Immediately refer the subpoena to the library's legal counsel.

- Counsel should examine the subpoena for any legal defect, including the manner in which it was served on the library, the breadth of its request, its form, or an insufficient showing of good cause made to a court. If a defect exists, counsel will advise on the best method to resist the subpoena.

- Through legal counsel, insist that any defect be cured before records are released and that the subpoena is strictly limited to require release of specifically identified records or documents. If there does not appear to be good cause for the subpoena, or if it seems too broad or intrusive, ask your attorney to file a motion to quash the subpoena in its entirety.

- Require that the agent, officer, or party requesting the information submit a new subpoena in good form and without defects.

- If you decide to comply with the subpoena after consulting with legal counsel, review the information that may be produced in response to the subpoena before releasing the information. Follow the subpoena strictly and do not provide any information that is not specifically requested in it.

- If disclosure is required, ask the court to enter a protective order (drafted by the library's counsel) keeping the information confidential and limiting its use to the particular case. Ask that access be restricted to those persons working directly on the case.

If the court order is in the form of a search warrant:

- Unlike a subpoena, a search warrant may be executed immediately. The agent or officer may begin a search of library records as soon as the library is served with the court's order.

- Ask to have library counsel present before the search begins in order to allow library counsel an opportunity to examine the search warrant and to ensure that the search conforms to the terms of the search warrant.

- If the officer refuses to delay the search, examine the warrant. Ensure that the warrant has been issued by a local or federal court in your state and is current and not expired. If you question the validity of the warrant, call the issuing court to confirm the validity of the warrant.

- The warrant will include information that identifies the premises to be searched and the items or records to be produced under the warrant. Ask that the officer observe the boundaries set by the search warrant.

- Cooperate with the search to ensure that only the records identified in the warrant are produced and that no other users' records are viewed or scanned.

Staff should be trained not to discuss the warrant with the officer, identify any documents, or to volunteer information without first consulting with the library's counsel.

- Record and keep an inventory of the records or items seized from the library. If possible, keep the originals and provide the agent with copies (or make copies for the library's reference).

- While most law enforcement officers will cooperate with a library's request to allow counsel to examine the warrant, it is possible that an officer will refuse to delay his or her search. Train staff to step aside and not to interfere with the officer in those cases. They should continue their attempt to notify the library director and library counsel, and make every effort to keep a record of the incident.

If the court order is a search warrant issued under the Foreign Intelligence Surveillance Act (FISA) (USA PATRIOT Act amendment):

- The recommendations for a regular search warrant still apply. However, a search warrant issued by a FISA court also contains a "gag order." That means that no person or institution served with the warrant can disclose that the warrant has been served or that records have been produced pursuant to the warrant.

- The library and its staff must comply with this order. No information can be disclosed to any other party, including the patron whose records are the subject of the search warrant. Note that the FSA gag order permits the person receiving the FISA warrant to inform the library director and those members of the staff who are needed to produce the records.

- The gag order does not change a library's right to legal representation during the search. The library can still seek legal advice concerning the warrant and request that the library's legal counsel be present during the actual search and execution of the warrant.

- If the library does not have legal counsel and wishes legal advice, the library can still obtain legal assistance through the Freedom to Read Foundation's legal counsel. Simply call the Office for Intellectual Freedom (800-545-2433, ext. 4223) and inform the staff that you need legal advice. OIF staff will ensure that an attorney returns your call. You do not have to and should not inform OIF staff of the existence of the warrant.

After the visit:

- Review the subpoena or search warrant with library counsel to ensure that the library complies with any remaining requirements, including restrictions on sharing information with others.

- Review library policies and staff response and make any necessary revisions in light of experience.

- Be prepared to communicate with the news media. Designate one person who will be responsible for communicating with the media. Develop a public information statement detailing the principles upholding library confidentiality that includes an explanation of the chilling effect on First Amendment rights caused by public access to users' personally identifiable information, and share it with your staff, so they are able to communicate the library's message to their acquaintances and neighbors in the community.

- If possible, notify the ALA about your experience by calling the Office for Intellectual Freedom at 800-545-2433, extension 4223.

Policy concerning Confidentiality of Personally Identifiable Information about Library Users

"In a library (physical or virtual), the right to privacy is the right to open inquiry without having the subject of one's interest examined or scrutinized by others. Confidentiality exists when a library is in possession of personally identifiable information about users and keeps that information private on their behalf" (*Privacy: An Interpretation of the Library Bill of Rights*).

The ethical responsibilities of librarians, as well as statutes in most states and the District of Columbia, protect the privacy of library users. Confidentiality extends to " information sought or received and resources consulted, borrowed, acquired or transmitted" (*ALA Code of Ethics*), and includes, but is not limited to, database search records, reference interviews, circulation records, interlibrary loan records and other personally identifiable uses of library materials, facilities, or services.

The First Amendment's guarantee of freedom of speech and of the press requires that the corresponding rights to hear what is spoken and read what is written be preserved, free from fear of government intrusion, intimidation, or repri-

sal. The American Library Association reaffirms its opposition to "any use of governmental prerogatives that lead to the intimidation of individuals or groups and discourages them from exercising the right of free expression as guaranteed by the First Amendment to the U.S. Constitution" and "encourages resistance to such abuse of governmental power . . ." (ALA Policy 53.4). In seeking access or in the pursuit of information, confidentiality is the primary means of providing the privacy that will free the individual from fear of intimidation or retaliation.

The American Library Association regularly receives reports of visits by agents of federal, state, and local law enforcement agencies to libraries, asking for personally identifiable information about library users. These visits, whether under the rubric of simply informing libraries of agency concerns or for some other reason, reflect an insensitivity to the legal and ethical bases for confidentiality, and the role it plays in the preservation of First Amendment rights, rights also extended to foreign nationals while in the United States. The government's interest in library use reflects a dangerous and fallacious equation of what a person reads with what that person believes or how that person is likely to behave. Such a presumption can and does threaten the freedom of access to information. It also is a threat to a crucial aspect of First Amendment rights: that freedom of speech and of the press include the freedom to hold, disseminate and receive unpopular, minority, extreme, or even dangerous ideas.

The American Library Association recognizes that law enforcement agencies and officers may occasionally believe that Library records contain information that would be helpful to the investigation of criminal activity. The American judicial system provides the mechanism for seeking release of such confidential records: a court order, following a showing of *good cause* based on *specific facts,* by a court of competent jurisdiction.

The American Library Association also recognizes that, under limited circumstances, access to certain information might be restricted due to a legitimate national security concern. However, there has been no showing of a plausible probability that national security will be compromised by any use made of unclassified information available in libraries. Access to this unclassified information should be handled no differently than access to any other information. Therefore, libraries and librarians have a legal and ethical responsibility to protect the confidentiality of all library users, including foreign nationals.

Libraries are one of the great bulwarks of democracy. They are living embodiments of the First Amendment because their collections include voices of dissent as well as assent. Libraries are impartial resources providing information on all points of view, available to all persons regardless of origin, age, background, or views. The role of libraries as such a resource must not be compromised by an erosion of the privacy rights of library users.

Adopted July 2, 1991, by the ALA Council; amended June 30, 2004.

Index